Thank you...

...for purchasing this copy of Homework Today for ages 8-9. We hope that you will find these 50 photocopiable worksheets helpful as part of your programme for homework activities. Each sheet is accompanied by an answer sheet. If you wish to, you can photocopy the answer sheets as well to enable your pupils to check their own work. Some sheets, of course, include questions where the answers will be completed in an individual way by the pupils.

Please note that photocopies can only be made for use by the purchasing institution; supplying copies to other schools, institutions or individuals breaches the copyright licence. Thank you for your help in this.

Overleaf we have drafted a letter which you may wish to photocopy, or amend, to send home to parents.

This Homework Today book is part of our growing range of educational titles. Most of our books are individual workbooks but, due to popular demand, we are now introducing a greater number of photocopiable titles especially for teachers. You may like to look out for:

Homework Today for ages 7- 8
Homework Today for ages 9-10
Homework Today for ages 10-11
Numeracy Today for ages 5-7
Numeracy Today for ages 7-9
Numeracy Today for ages 9-11
Best Handwriting for ages 7-11
Spelling for Literacy (set of five books providing a complete spelling course for ages 5-11)

To find details of our other publications, please visit our website: www.acblack.com

Dear Parents,

We are pleased to be providing homework sheets for our eight to nine year old pupils, from a book called 'Homework Today'. These sheets contain activities which will enable your child to revise some of the skills and knowledge which they have acquired at school. The amount of time taken to complete each sheet will vary considerably but, as a guide, you should allow approximately 15 to 20 minutes per homework.

Try to help your child 'get into the homework habit' by providing a quiet place to work, with a desk or a table. Encourage your child to work in pen for written work and in pencil for maths. Neat presentation is important and reflects the pride your child takes in producing good quality work.

Thank you for supporting the work of the school by encouraging your child with homework.

Yours sincerely,

Homework Today is published by Andrew Brodie Publications.
Andrew Brodie Publications publish a range of educational workbooks for children, available through bookstores or through the website: **www.acblack.com**

CONTENTS PAGE

Homework Today is published by Andrew Brodie Publications.
Andrew Brodie Publications publish a range of educational workbooks for children, available through bookstores or through the website: **www.acblack.com**

Number

1

Homework Today

Name: Date:

Words and Numbers

Match the words to the numbers.

two thousand, four hundred and sixteen	398
three hundred and ninety-eight	5150
one thousand, seven hundred and fifty	6042
five thousand, one hundred and fifty	2416
nine hundred and thirty-eight	4062
six hundred and forty-two	1750
four thousand and sixty-two	938
six thousand and forty-two	642

Now write the words for these numbers.

214 ➔

4120 ➔

2140 ➔

1420 ➔

4210 ➔

63 ➔

633 ➔

6333 ➔

3336 ➔

3006 ➔

Homework Today **Answer Sheet**

Number **1**

Name: Date:

Words and Numbers

Match the words to the numbers.

two thousand, four hundred and sixteen	398
three hundred and ninety-eight	5150
one thousand, seven hundred and fifty	6042
five thousand, one hundred and fifty	2416
nine hundred and thirty-eight	4062
six hundred and forty-two	1750
four thousand and sixty-two	938
six thousand and forty-two	642

Now write the words for these numbers.

214	→	two hundred and fourteen
4120	→	four thousand, one hundred and twenty
2140	→	two thousand, one hundred and forty
1420	→	one thousand, four hundred and twenty
4210	→	four thousand, two hundred and ten
63	→	sixty-three
633	→	six hundred and thirty-three
6333	→	six thousand, three hundred and thirty-three
3336	→	three thousand, three hundred and thirty-six
3006	→	three thousand and six

Homework Today

Name: Date:

Numbers in Order

Put the numbers in each set in order. Start with the smallest number.

Set A	43	18	89	21	50	6
Set B	306	603	360	613	136	630
Set C	2114	1142	4211	1412	2411	2141

Now write the numbers in the sets below in the correct order. This time, start with the largest number.

Set D	91	58	17	63	94	39
Set E	219	527	725	275	192	752
Set F	3001	1003	3100	1300	1113	1311

Homework Today — Answer Sheet

Number 2

Name: Date:

Numbers in Order

Put the numbers in each set in order. Start with the smallest number.

Set A	43	18	89	21	50	6
	6	18	21	43	50	89
Set B	306	603	360	613	136	630
	136	306	360	603	613	630
Set C	2114	1142	4211	1412	2411	2141
	1142	1412	2114	2141	2411	4211

Now write the numbers in the sets below in the correct order. This time, start with the largest number.

Set D	91	58	17	63	94	39
	94	91	63	58	39	17
Set E	219	527	725	275	192	752
	752	725	527	275	219	192
Set F	3001	1003	3100	1300	1113	1311
	3100	3001	1311	1300	1113	1003

Number 3

Homework Today

Name: Date:

Number Lines

Look carefully at the number lines.

Write the correct numbers in the boxes.

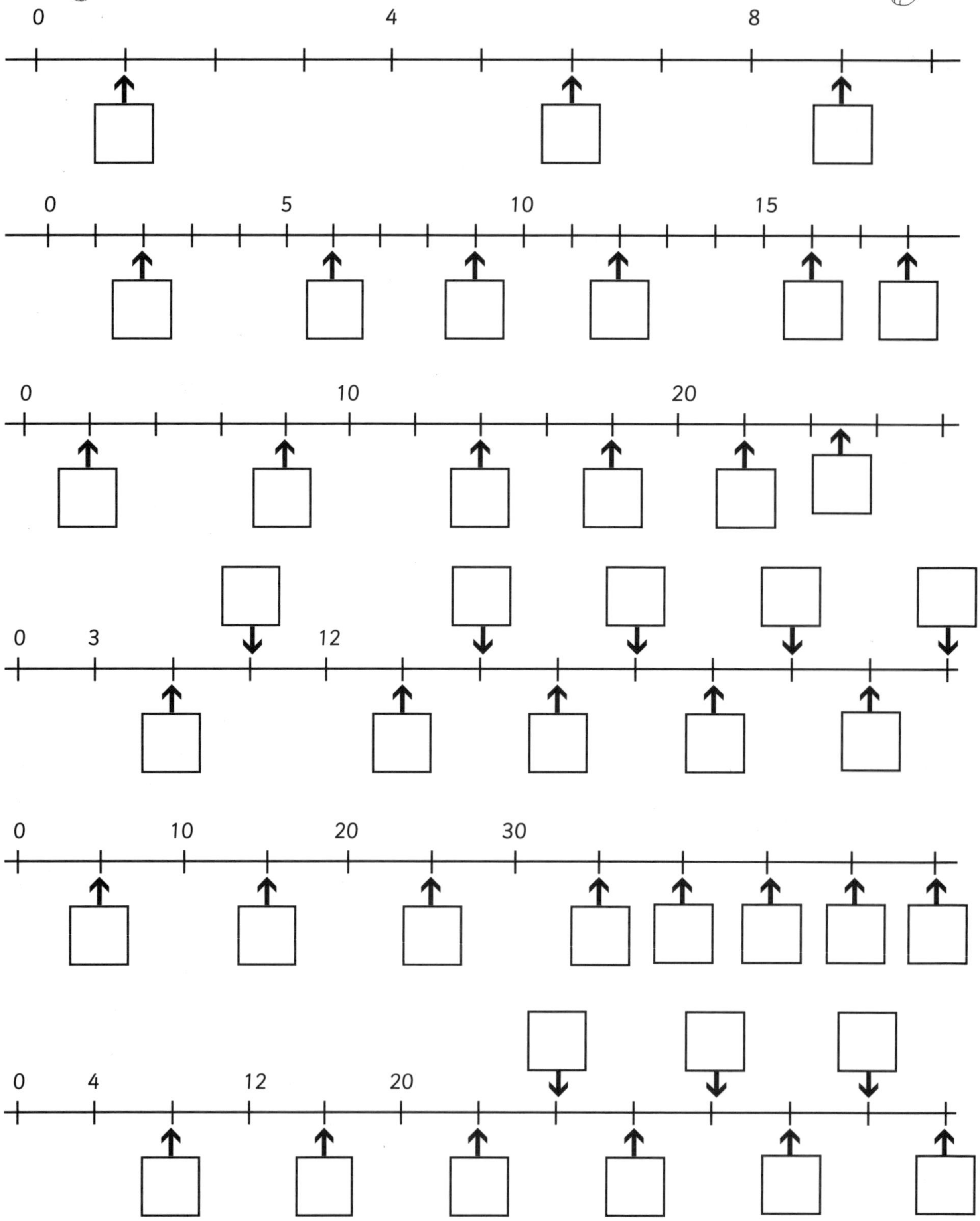

Homework Today — Answer Sheet

Number 3

Name: Date:

Number Lines

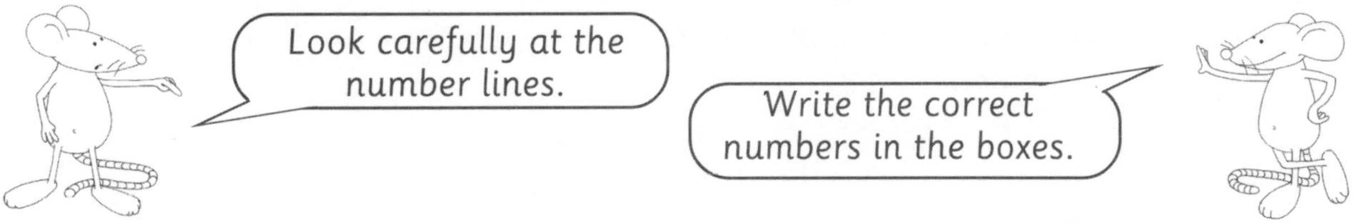

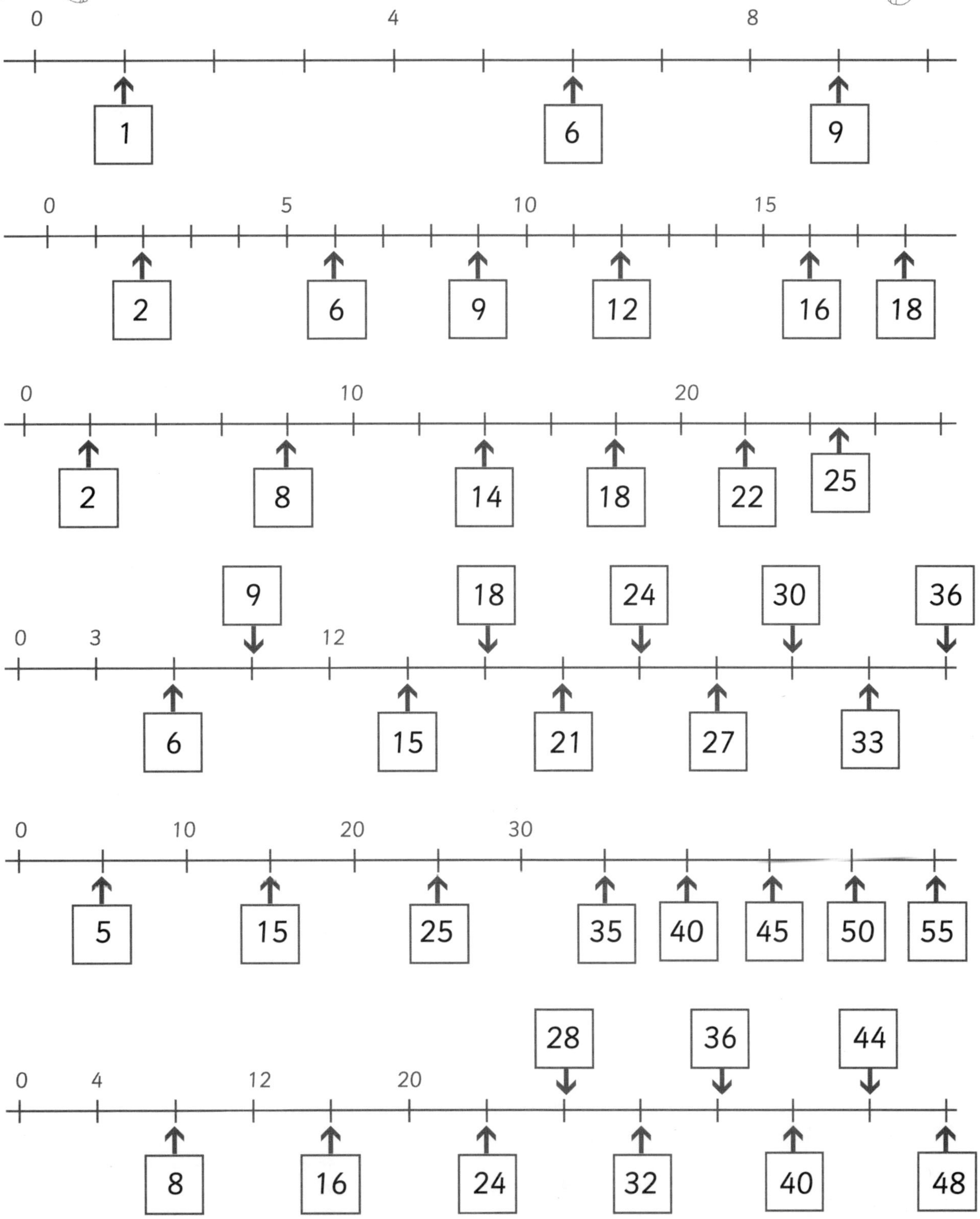

Number 4

Homework Today

Name: Date:

Positive and Negative

Look very carefully at the number lines.

Write the correct numbers in the boxes.

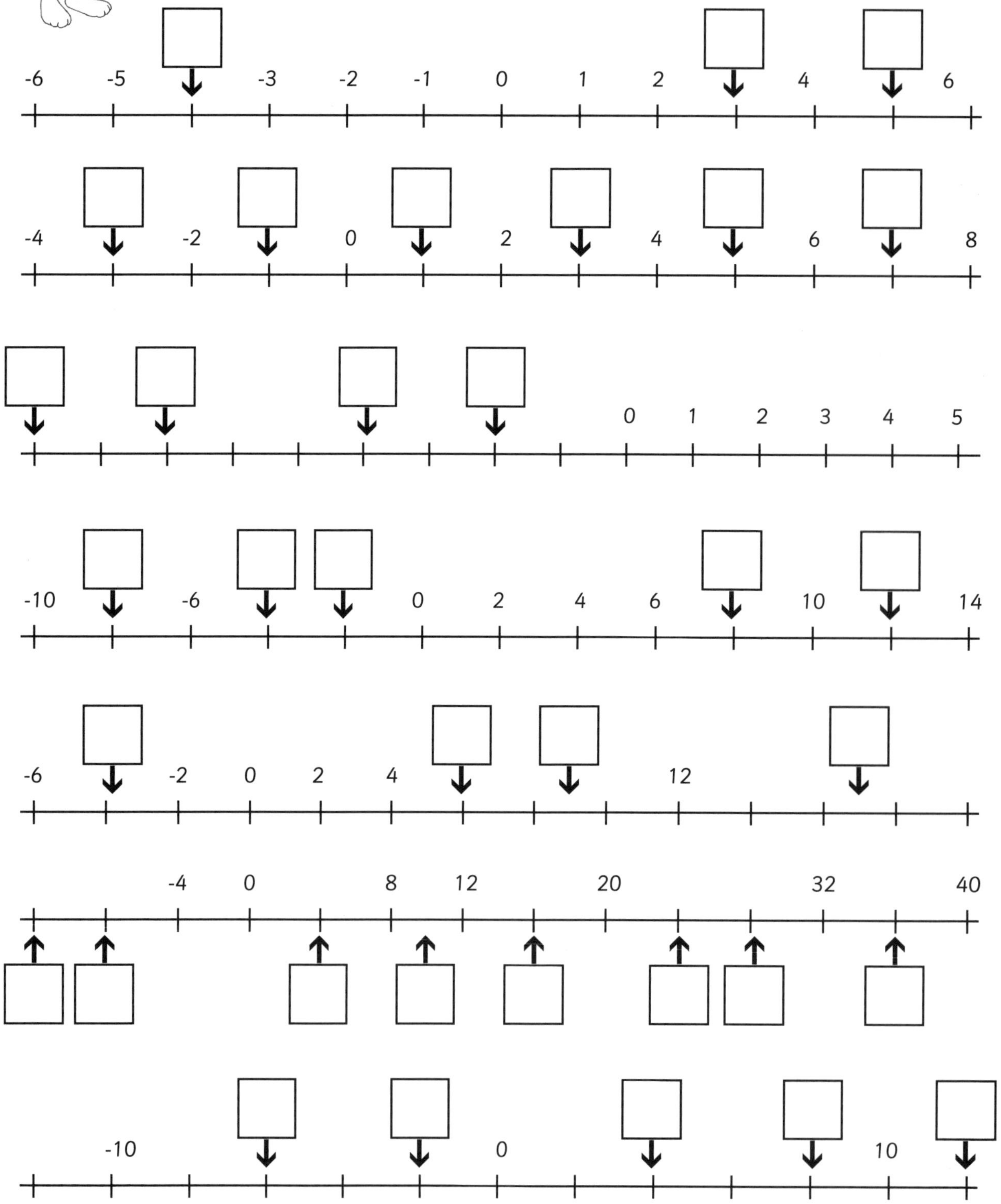

Homework Today

Answer Sheet

Number 4

Name: Date:

Positive and Negative

Look very carefully at the number lines.

Write the correct number the boxes.

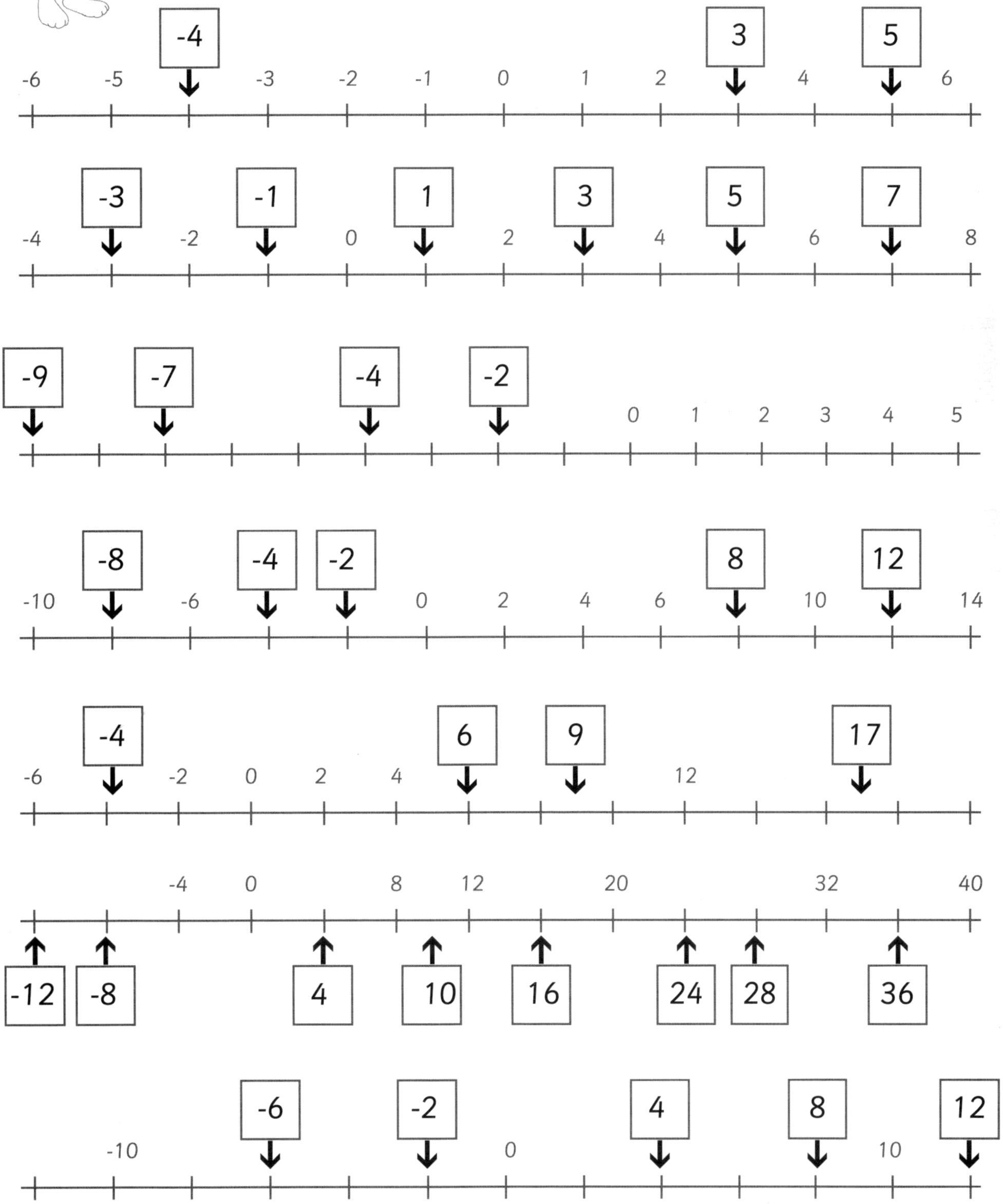

Number

5

Homework Today

Name: Date:

Addition Bonds

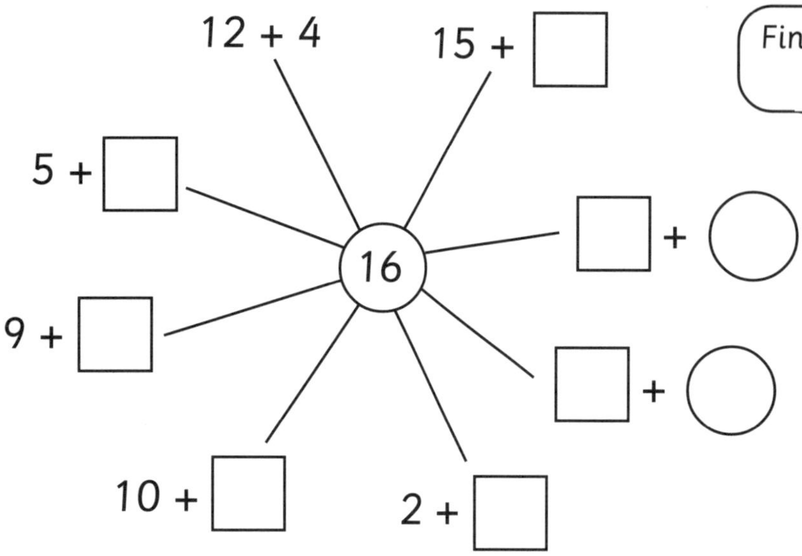

Find some additions for each of these number spiders.

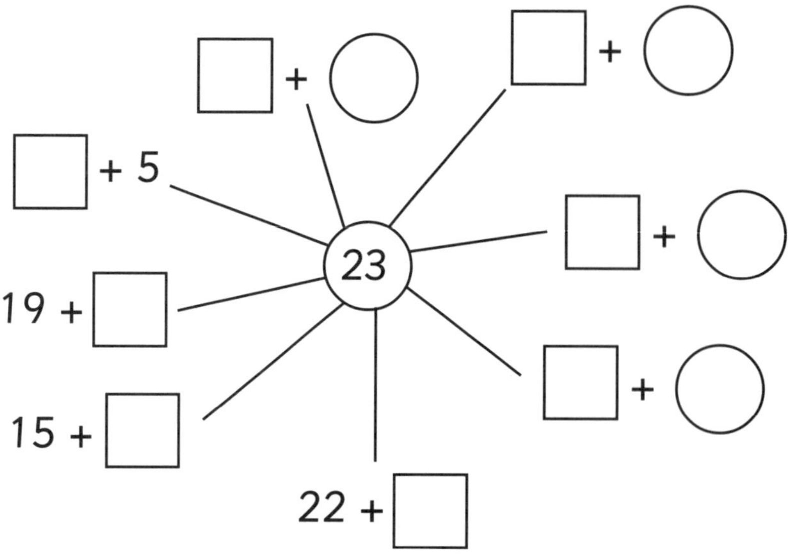

You must only use whole numbers.

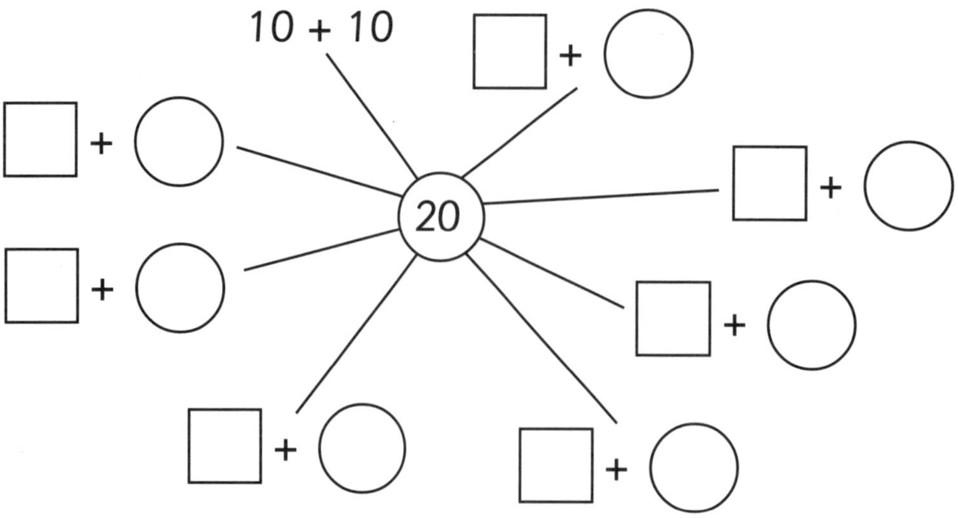

Homework Today — Answer Sheet

Number **5**

Name: Date:

Addition Bonds

Find some additions for each of these number spiders.

16

- 12 + 4
- 15 + 1
- 5 + 11
- 8 + 8
- 9 + 7
- 3 + 13
- 10 + 6
- 2 + 14

You must only use whole numbers.

23

- 3 + 20
- 6 + 17
- 18 + 5
- 13 + 10
- 19 + 4
- 7 + 16
- 15 + 8
- 22 + 1

20

- 10 + 10
- 1 + 19
- 15 + 5
- 13 + 7
- 4 + 16
- 17 + 3
- 11 + 9
- 20 + 0

Number

6

Homework Today

Name: Date:

Quick Subtractions

Solve these subtractions as quickly as you can.

12 - 6 = □

17 - 9 = □

13 - 7 = □

16 - 3 = □

26 -13 = □

36 - 29 = □

36 - 23 = □

14 - 8 = □

15 - 7 = □

11 - 4 = □

14 - 9 = □

34 -29 = □

44 - 39 = □

50 - 39 = □

13 - □ = 9

17 - □ = 8

15 - □ = 12

Try these questions.

23 - □ = 19

14 - □ = 5

15 - □ = 8

33 - □ = 29

12 - □ = 4

15 - □ = 3

Now choose your own ways to make these questions true.

□ - △ = 12

□ - △ = 4

□ - △ = 20

□ - △ = 6

□ - △ = 18

□ - △ = 14

Homework Today — Answer Sheet

Number 6

Name: Date:

Quick Subtractions

Solve these subtractions as quickly as you can.

12 - 6 = 6	14 - 8 = 6
17 - 9 = 8	15 - 7 = 8
13 - 7 = 6	11 - 4 = 7
16 - 3 = 13	14 - 9 = 5
26 -13 = 13	34 -29 = 5
36 - 29 = 7	44 - 39 = 5
36 - 23 = 13	50 - 39 = 11

13 - 4 = 9

17 - 9 = 8

15 - 3 = 12

Try these questions.

23 - 4 = 19	33 - 4 = 29
14 - 9 = 5	12 - 8 = 4
15 - 7 = 8	15 - 12 = 3

Now choose your own ways to make these questions true.

Different answers are possible.

9 - 3 = 6	14 - 2 = 12
50 - 32 = 18	8 - 4 = 4
	48 - 28 = 20
	17 - 3 = 14

Homework Today

Name: Date:

Addition Pairs

Look at the ways we can make 12 by adding pairs of whole numbers.

Now find all the addition pairs for the numbers below.

12

1 + 11 = 12	11 + 1 = 12
2 + 10 = 12	10 + 2 = 12
3 + 9 = 12	9 + 3 = 12
4 + 8 = 12	8 + 4 = 12
5 + 7 = 12	7 + 5 = 12

6 + 6 = 12

10

1 + 9 = 10	9 + 1 = 10

11

1 + 10 = 11	10 + 1 = 11

13

1 + 12 = 13	12 + 1 = 13

14

1 + 13 = 14	13 + 1 = 14

Homework Today — Answer Sheet

Number 7

Name: Date:

Addition Pairs

Look at the ways we can make 12 by adding pairs of whole numbers.

Now find all the addition pairs for the numbers below.

12

1 + 11 = 12	11 + 1 = 12
2 + 10 = 12	10 + 2 = 12
3 + 9 = 12	9 + 3 = 12
4 + 8 = 12	8 + 4 = 12
5 + 7 = 12	7 + 5 = 12
6 + 6 = 12	

10

1 + 9 = 10	9 + 1 = 10
2 + 8 = 10	8 + 2 = 10
3 + 7 = 10	7 + 3 = 10
4 + 6 = 10	6 + 4 = 10
5 + 5 = 10	

11

1 + 10 = 11	10 + 1 = 11
2 + 9 = 11	9 + 2 = 11
3 + 8 = 11	8 + 3 = 11
4 + 7 = 11	7 + 4 = 11
5 + 6 = 11	6 + 5 = 11

13

1 + 12 = 13	12 + 1 = 13
2 + 11 = 13	11 + 2 = 13
3 + 10 = 13	10 + 3 = 13
4 + 9 = 13	9 + 4 = 13
5 + 8 = 13	8 + 5 = 13
6 + 7 = 13	7 + 6 = 13

14

1 + 13 = 14	13 + 1 = 14
2 + 12 = 14	12 + 2 = 14
3 + 11 = 14	11 + 3 = 14
4 + 10 = 14	10 + 4 = 14
5 + 9 = 14	9 + 5 = 14
6 + 8 = 14	8 + 6 = 14
7 + 7 = 14	

Number

8

Homework Today

Name: Date:

More Addition Pairs

Find all the addition pairs for the numbers shown.

15

1 + 14 = 15	14 + 1 = 15

16

1 + 15 = 16	15 + 1 = 16

17

1 + 16 = 17	16 + 1 = 17

18

On the back of the sheet, write all the addition pairs for 19 and for 20.

Homework Today   Answer Sheet

Number **8**

Name: Date:

More Addition Pairs

Find all the addition pairs for the numbers shown.

(15)

1 + 14 = 15	14 + 1 = 15
2 + 13 = 15	13 + 2 = 15
3 + 12 = 15	12 + 3 = 15
4 + 11 = 15	11 + 4 = 15
5 + 10 = 15	10 + 5 = 15
6 + 9 = 15	9 + 6 = 15
7 + 8 = 15	8 + 7 = 15

(16)

1 + 15 = 16	15 + 1 = 16
2 + 14 = 16	14 + 2 = 16
3 + 13 = 16	13 + 3 = 16
4 + 12 = 16	12 + 4 = 16
5 + 11 = 16	11 + 5 = 16
6 + 10 = 16	10 + 6 = 16
7 + 9 = 16	9 + 7 = 16

8 + 8 = 16

(17)

1 + 16 = 17	16 + 1 = 17
2 + 15 = 17	15 + 2 = 17
3 + 14 = 17	14 + 3 = 17
4 + 13 = 17	13 + 4 = 17
5 + 12 = 17	12 + 5 = 17
6 + 11 = 17	11 + 6 = 17
7 + 10 = 17	10 + 7 = 17
8 + 9 = 17	9 + 8 = 17

(18)

1 + 17 = 18	17 + 1 = 18
2 + 16 = 18	16 + 2 = 18
3 + 15 = 18	15 + 3 = 18
4 + 14 = 18	14 + 4 = 18
5 + 13 = 18	13 + 5 = 18
6 + 12 = 18	12 + 6 = 18
7 + 11 = 18	11 + 7 = 18
8 + 10 = 18	10 + 8 = 18

9 + 9 = 18

On the back of the sheet, write all the addition pairs for 19 and for 20.

Number

9

Homework Today

Name: Date:

Quick Doubles

Look: 25 + 25 = 50

2 x 25 = 50

double 25 = 50

Time yourself answering each set of questions below.

Set A	Set B	Set C
3 + 3 =	2 x 10 =	double 8 =
7 + 3 =	2 x 5 =	double 1 =
1 + 1 =	2 x 9 =	double 3 =
4 + 4 =	2 x 6 =	double 13 =
5 + 5 =	2 x 7 =	double 2 =
8 + 8 =	2 x 12 =	double 5 =
2 + 2 =	2 x 8 =	double 9 =
6 + 6 =	2 x 3 =	double 4 =
10 + 10 =	2 x 11 =	double 6 =
9 + 9 =	2 x 2 =	double 12 =
12 + 12 =	2 x 4 =	double 7 =
11 + 11 =	2 x 13 =	double 10 =
13 + 13 =	2 x 1 =	double 11 =

Homework Today — Answer Sheet

Number 9

Name: Date:

Quick Doubles

Look:

25 + 25 = 50
2 x 25 = 50
double 25 = 50

Time yourself answering each set of questions below.

Set A		Set B		Set C	
3 + 3 =	6	2 x 10 =	20	double 8 =	16
7 + 3 =	10	2 x 5 =	10	double 1 =	2
1 + 1 =	2	2 x 9 =	18	double 3 =	6
4 + 4 =	8	2 x 6 =	12	double 13 =	26
5 + 5 =	10	2 x 7 =	14	double 2 =	4
8 + 8 =	16	2 x 12 =	24	double 5 =	10
2 + 2 =	4	2 x 8 =	16	double 9 =	18
6 + 6 =	12	2 x 3 =	6	double 4 =	8
10 + 10 =	20	2 x 11 =	22	double 6 =	12
9 + 9 =	18	2 x 2 =	4	double 12 =	24
12 + 12 =	24	2 x 4 =	8	double 7 =	14
11 + 11 =	22	2 x 13 =	26	double 10 =	20
13 + 13 =	26	2 x 1 =	2	double 11 =	22

Number 10

Homework Today

Name: Date:

More Doubles

Answer these doubles as quickly as you can.

double 10 = ☐	double 20 = ☐
double 30 = ☐	double 40 = ☐
double 50 = ☐	double 60 = ☐
double 70 = ☐	double 80 = ☐
double 90 = ☐	double 100 = ☐

Look at double 37:

37 → double 30 = 60 and double 7 = 14

60 + 14 = 74

Try to solve these doubles.

double 15 = ☐	double 18 = ☐	double 23 = ☐
double 21 = ☐	double 32 = ☐	double 27 = ☐
double 43 = ☐	double 19 = ☐	double 26 = ☐
double 49 = ☐	double 17 = ☐	double 28 = ☐
double 25 = ☐	double 39 = ☐	double 34 = ☐

Homework Today   Answer Sheet

Number 10

Name: Date:

More Doubles

Answer these doubles as quickly as you can.

double 10 = 20	double 20 = 40
double 30 = 60	double 40 = 80
double 50 = 100	double 60 = 120
double 70 = 140	double 80 = 160
double 90 = 180	double 100 = 200

Look at double 37:

37 → double 30 = 60 and double 7 = 14

60 + 14 = 74

Try to solve these doubles.

double 15 = 30	double 18 = 36	double 23 = 46
double 21 = 42	double 32 = 64	double 27 = 54
double 43 = 86	double 19 = 38	double 26 = 52
double 49 = 98	double 17 = 34	double 28 = 56
double 25 = 50	double 39 = 78	double 34 = 68

Number

11

Homework Today

Name: Date:

Quick Halves

Look:

$40 \div 2 = 20$

$^1/_2$ of $40 = 20$

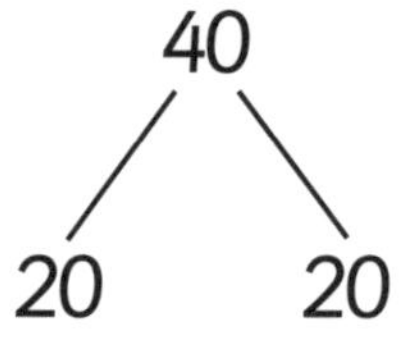

Try these halving questions:

$^1/_2$ of 16 = ☐	$^1/_2$ of 24 = ☐	$^1/_2$ of 30 = ☐
$^1/_2$ of 50 = ☐	$^1/_2$ of 60 = ☐	$^1/_2$ of 18 = ☐
$^1/_2$ of 20 = ☐	$^1/_2$ of 26 = ☐	$^1/_2$ of 36 = ☐

Quick Quarters

Look:

$40 \div 4 = 10$

$^1/_4$ of $40 = 10$

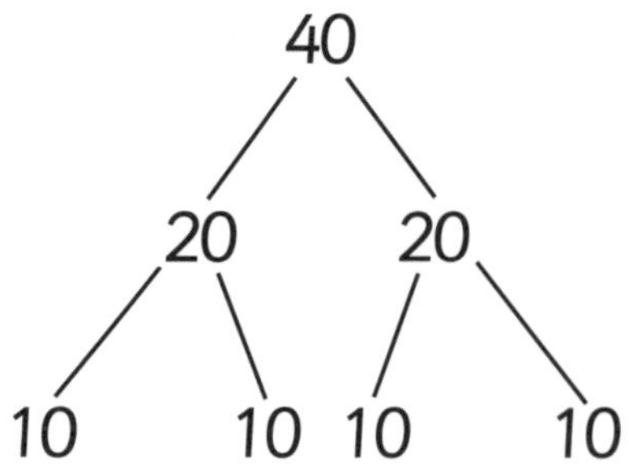

Try these questions:

$^1/_4$ of 8 = ☐	$^1/_4$ of 12 = ☐	$^1/_4$ of 20 = ☐
$^1/_4$ of 16 = ☐	$^1/_4$ of 24 = ☐	$^1/_4$ of 32 = ☐
$^1/_4$ of 80 = ☐	$^1/_4$ of 36 = ☐	$^1/_4$ of 28 = ☐

Homework Today Answer Sheet

Number 11

Name: Date:

Quick Halves

Look:

$40 \div 2 = 20$

$^1/_2$ of $40 = 20$

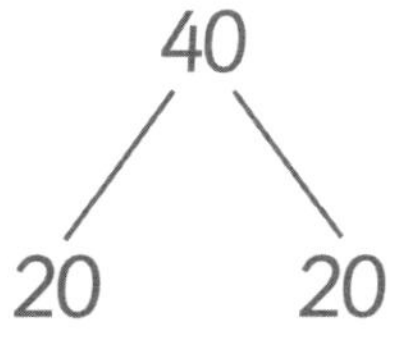

Try these halving questions:

$^1/_2$ of 16 = 8	$^1/_2$ of 24 = 12	$^1/_2$ of 30 = 15
$^1/_2$ of 50 = 25	$^1/_2$ of 60 = 30	$^1/_2$ of 18 = 9
$^1/_2$ of 20 = 10	$^1/_2$ of 26 = 13	$^1/_2$ of 36 = 18

Quick Quarters

Look:

$40 \div 4 = 10$

$^1/_4$ of $40 = 10$

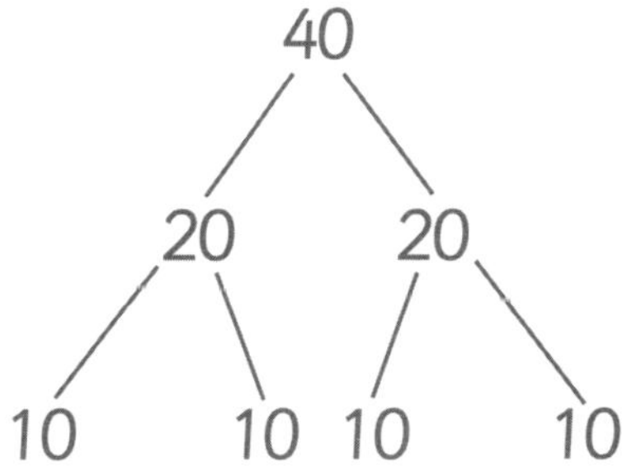

Try these questions:

$^1/_4$ of 8 = 2	$^1/_4$ of 12 = 3	$^1/_4$ of 20 = 5
$^1/_4$ of 16 = 4	$^1/_4$ of 24 = 6	$^1/_4$ of 32 = 8
$^1/_4$ of 80 = 20	$^1/_4$ of 36 = 9	$^1/_4$ of 28 = 7

Number 12

Homework Today

Name: Date:

Shapes and Perimeters

Write the correct name on each shape.

WORD BANK

triangle parallelogram
rectangle pentagon
square hexagon

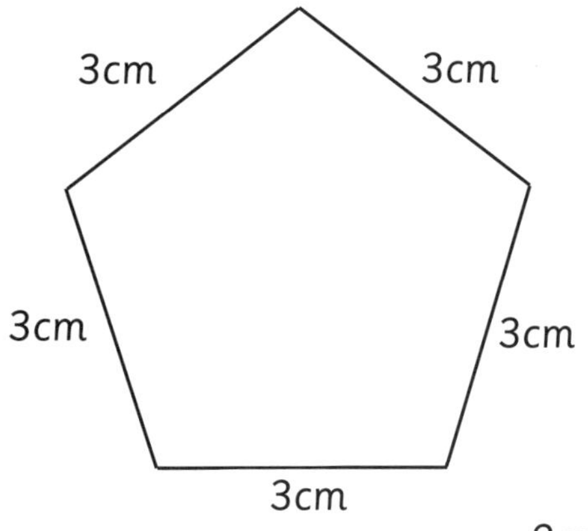

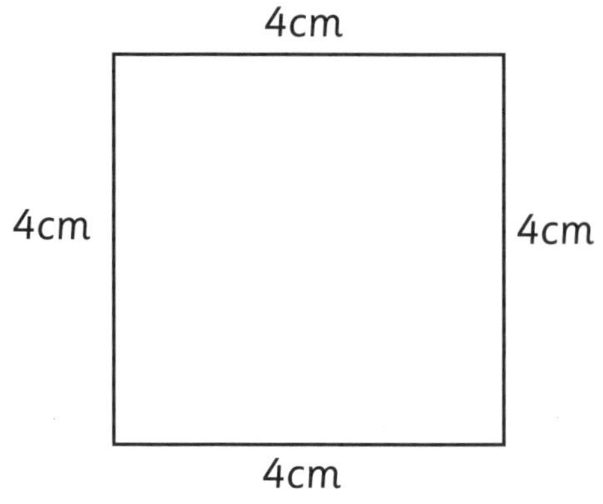

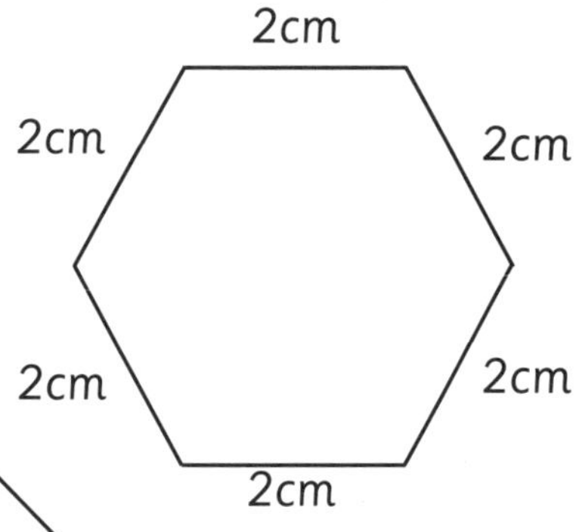

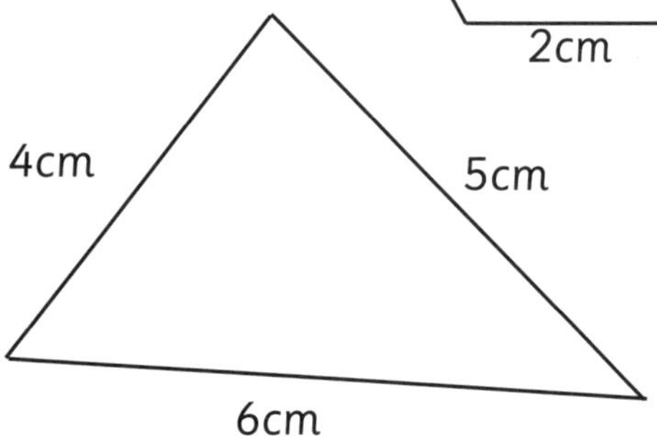

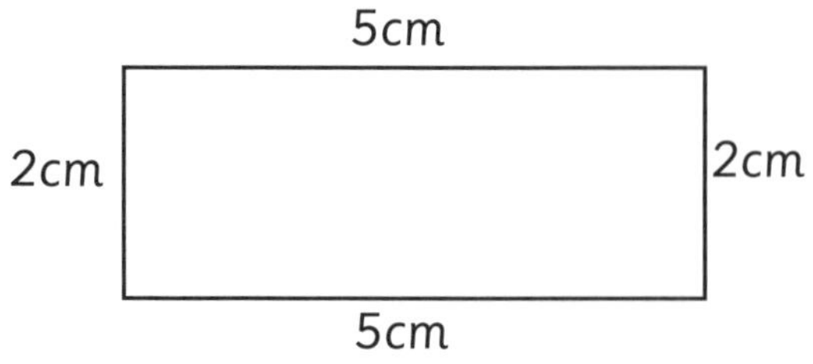

The perimeter of the triangle is ☐

The perimeter of the square is ☐

The perimeter of the pentagon is ☐

The perimeter of the rectangle is ☐

The perimeter of the hexagon is ☐

The perimeter of the parallelogram is ☐

Homework Today Answer Sheet

Number 12

Name: Date:

Shapes and Perimeters

Write the correct name on each shape.

WORD BANK

triangle parallelogram
rectangle pentagon
square hexagon

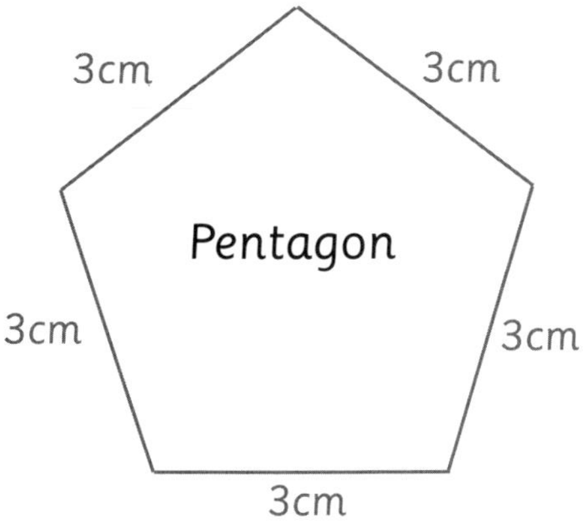

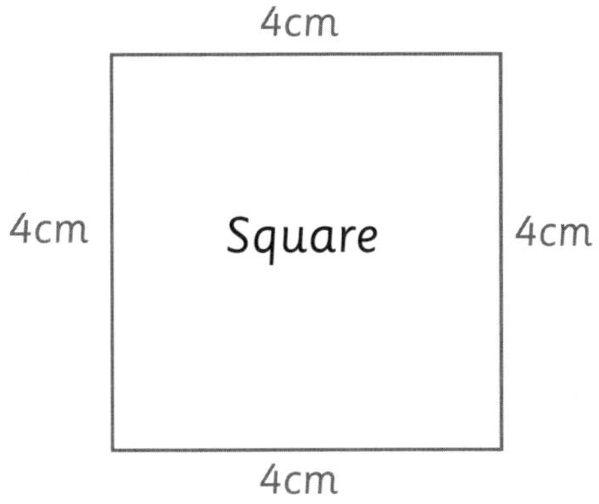

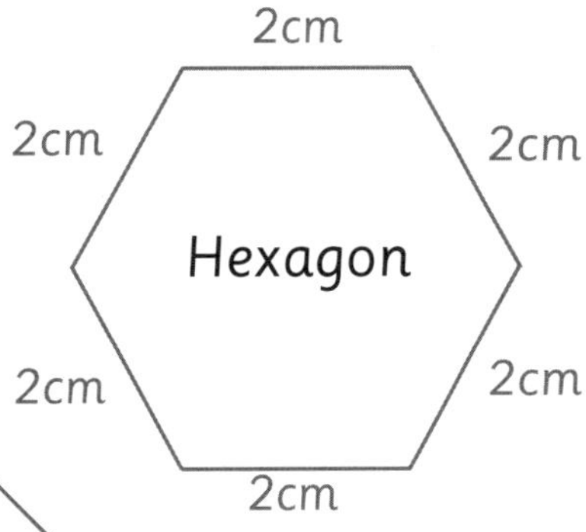

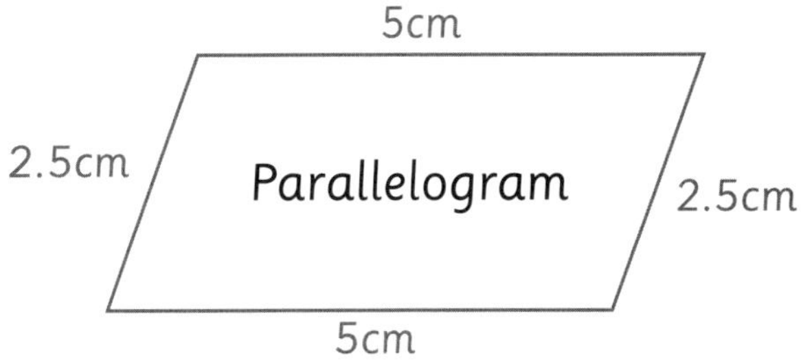

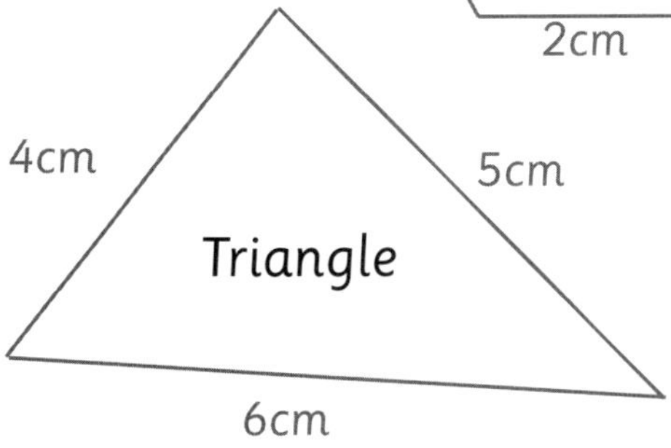

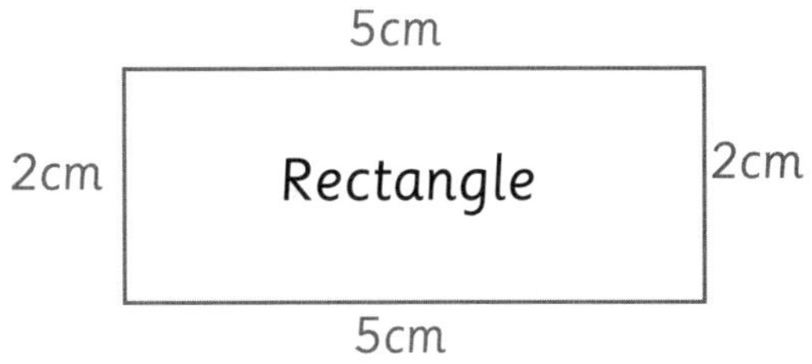

The perimeter of the triangle is	15 cm
The perimeter of the square is	16 cm
The perimeter of the pentagon is	15 cm
The perimeter of the rectangle is	14 cm
The perimeter of the hexagon is	12 cm
The perimeter of the parallelogram is	15 cm

Number

13

Homework Today

Name: Date:

Using a Ruler

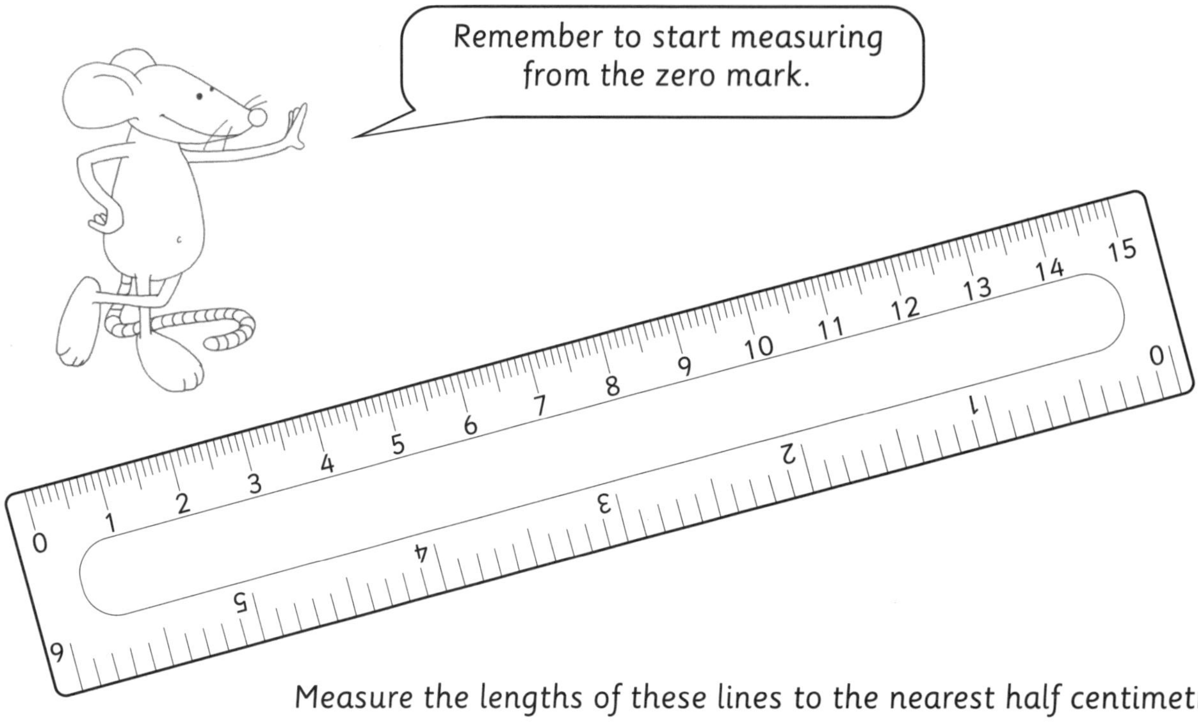

Measure the lengths of these lines to the nearest half centimetre.

________________________	cm
____________________	cm
__________________________________	cm
___________________________	cm
_______	cm
_________________	cm
____________________________	cm
________________________________	cm
______________________	cm

On the back of the sheet draw, accurately, lines of these sizes:

4 cm $\quad$ $4\,^1/_2$ cm $\quad$ 3 cm $\quad$ 9 cm $\quad$ 11 cm

Homework Today **Answer Sheet** Number 13

Name: Date:

Using a Ruler

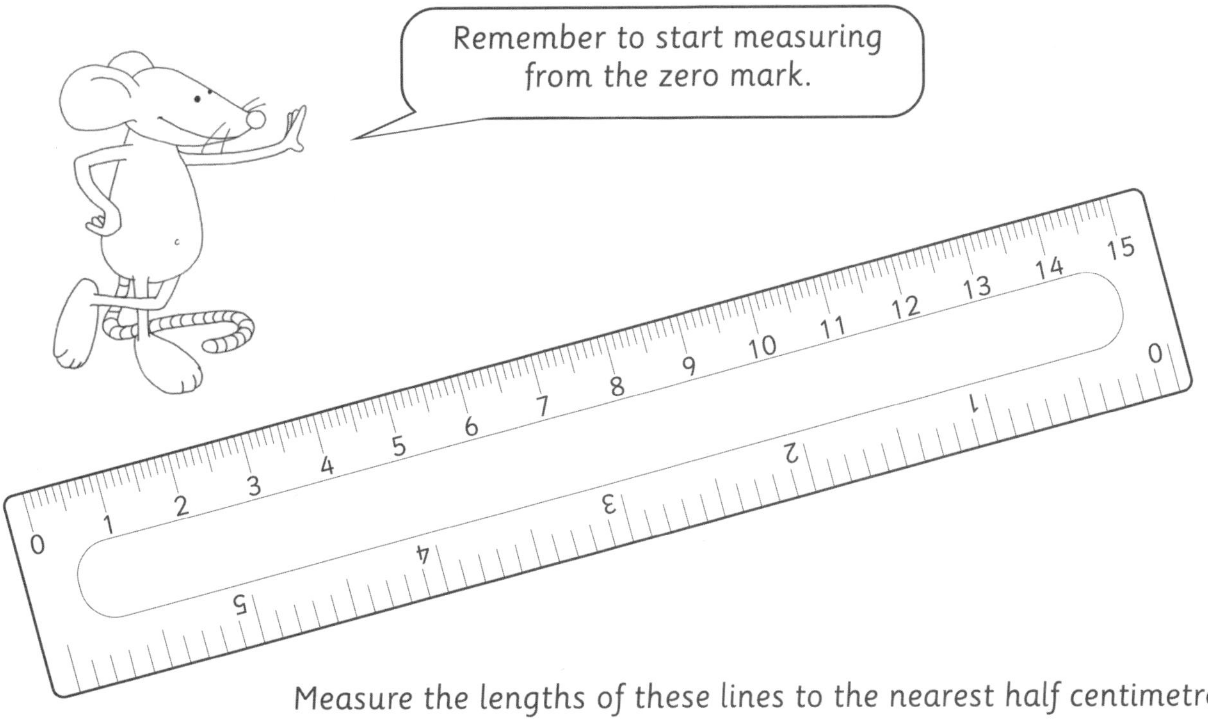

Measure the lengths of these lines to the nearest half centimetre.

$8\frac{1}{2}$ cm
7 cm
12 cm
$9\frac{1}{2}$ cm
$2\frac{1}{2}$ cm
6 cm
10 cm
$11\frac{1}{2}$ cm
8 cm

On the back of the sheet draw, accurately, lines of these sizes:

4 cm $4\frac{1}{2}$ cm   3 cm   9 cm   11 cm

Number 14

Homework Today

Name: Date:

Using Measuring Cylinders

How much water is in each measuring cylinder?

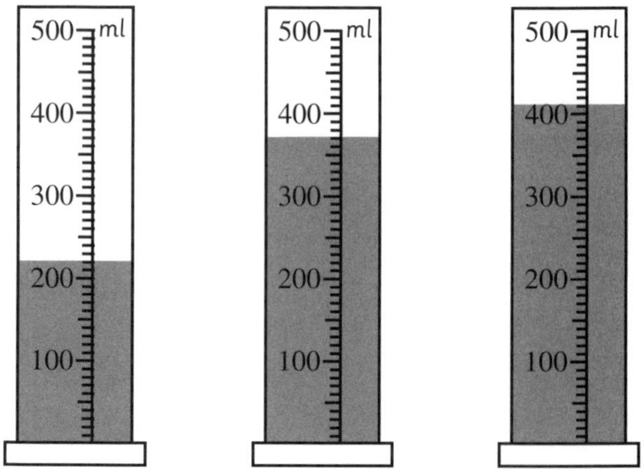

(a) ☐ (b) ☐ (c) ☐

What is the difference in quantity between the water in cylinder **d** and the water in cylinder *f*? ☐

If we poured all the water from these six cylinders into one bowl, how much water would be in the bowl? ☐

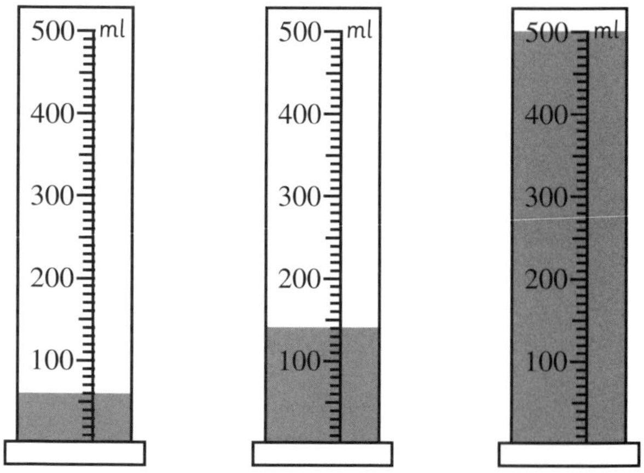

(d) ☐ (e) ☐ (f) ☐

Draw water in the measuring cylinders below, to the measurements given.

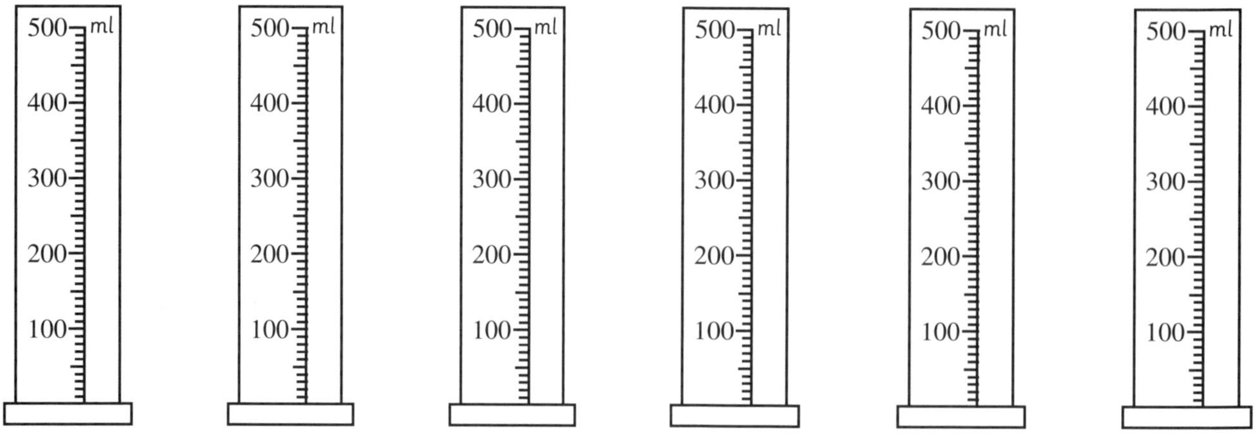

(g) 90 ml (h) 300 ml (i) 250 ml (j) 480 ml (k) 70 ml (l) 180 ml

Homework Today Answer Sheet

Number 14

Name: Date:

Using Measuring Cylinders

How much water is in each measuring cylinder?

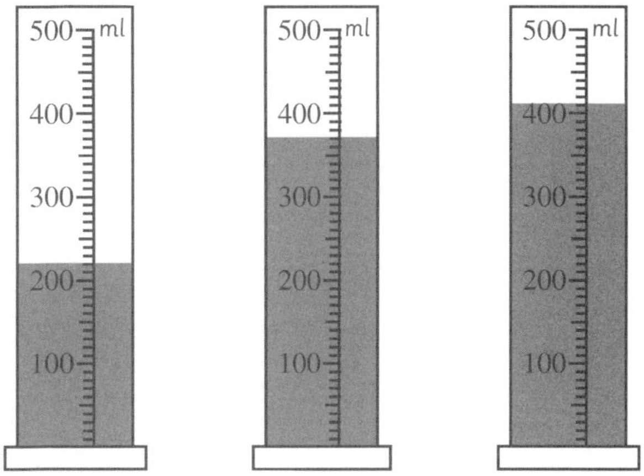

(a) 220 ml (b) 370 ml (c) 410 ml

What is the difference in quantity between the water in cylinder **d** and the water in cylinder *f*?

440 ml

If we poured all the water from these six cylinders into one bowl, how much water would be in the bowl?

1700 ml

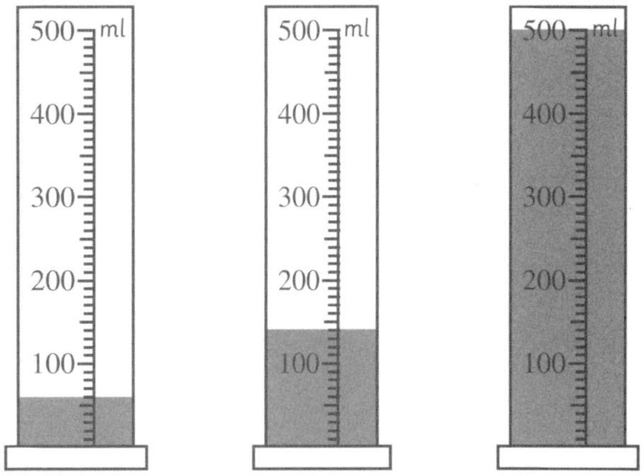

(d) 60 ml (e) 140 ml (f) 500 ml

Draw water in the measuring cylinders below, to the measurements given.

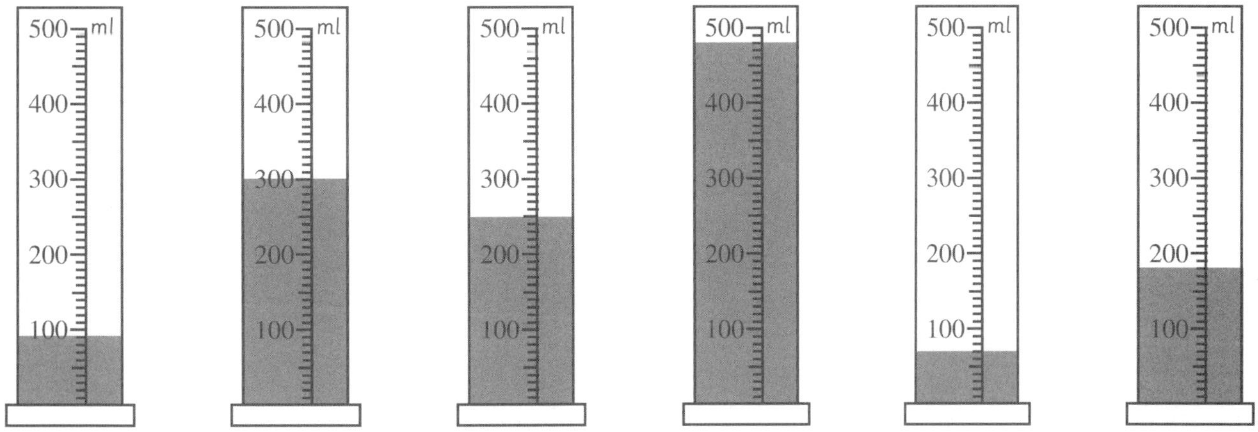

(g) 90 ml (h) 300 ml (i) 250 ml (j) 480 ml (k) 70 ml (l) 180 ml

Number

15

Homework Today

Name: Date:

Area

Count the squares to find the area of each shape. Sometimes there are half-squares.

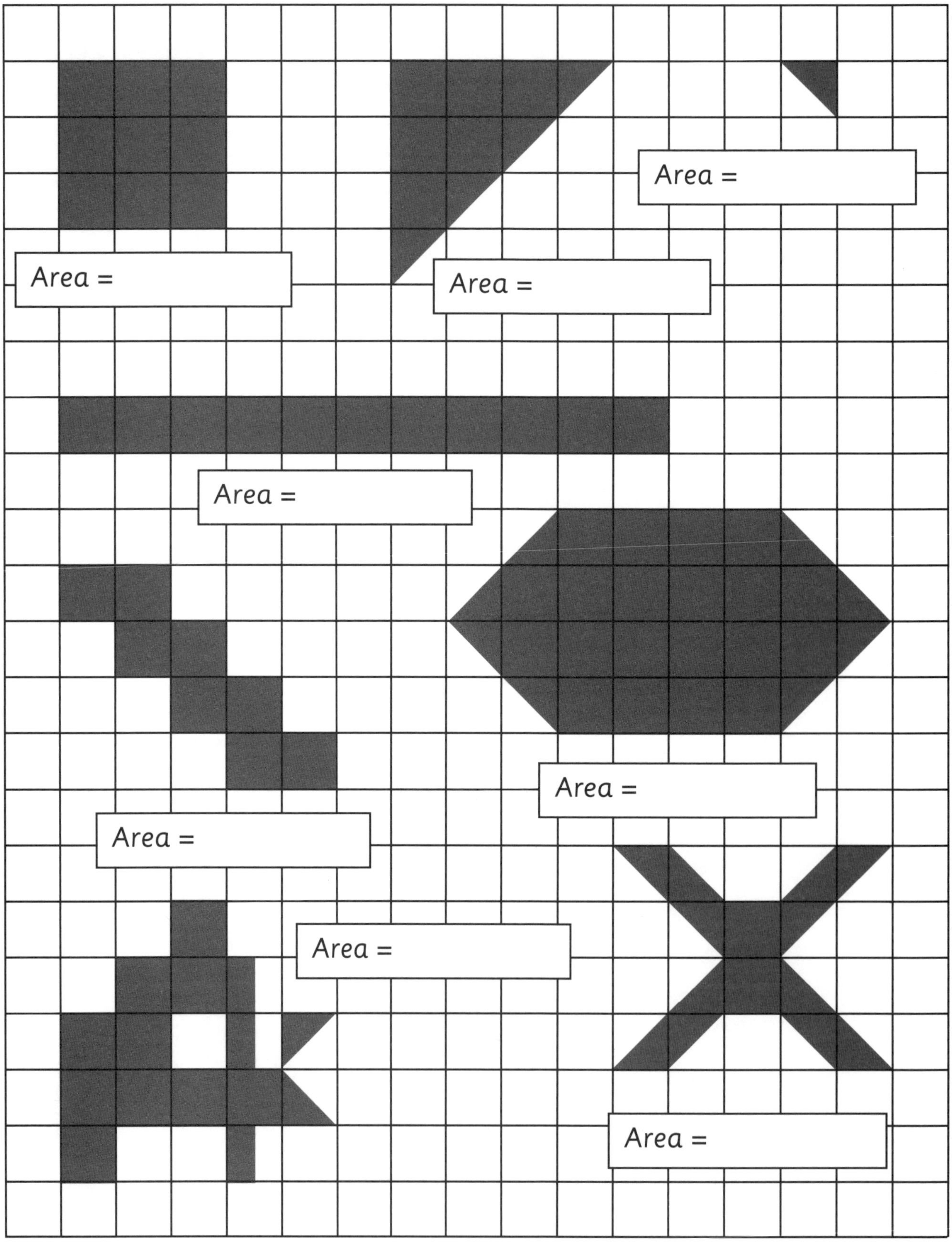

Homework Today **Answer Sheet** Number 15

Name: Date:

Area

Count the squares to find the area of each shape. Sometimes there are half-squares.

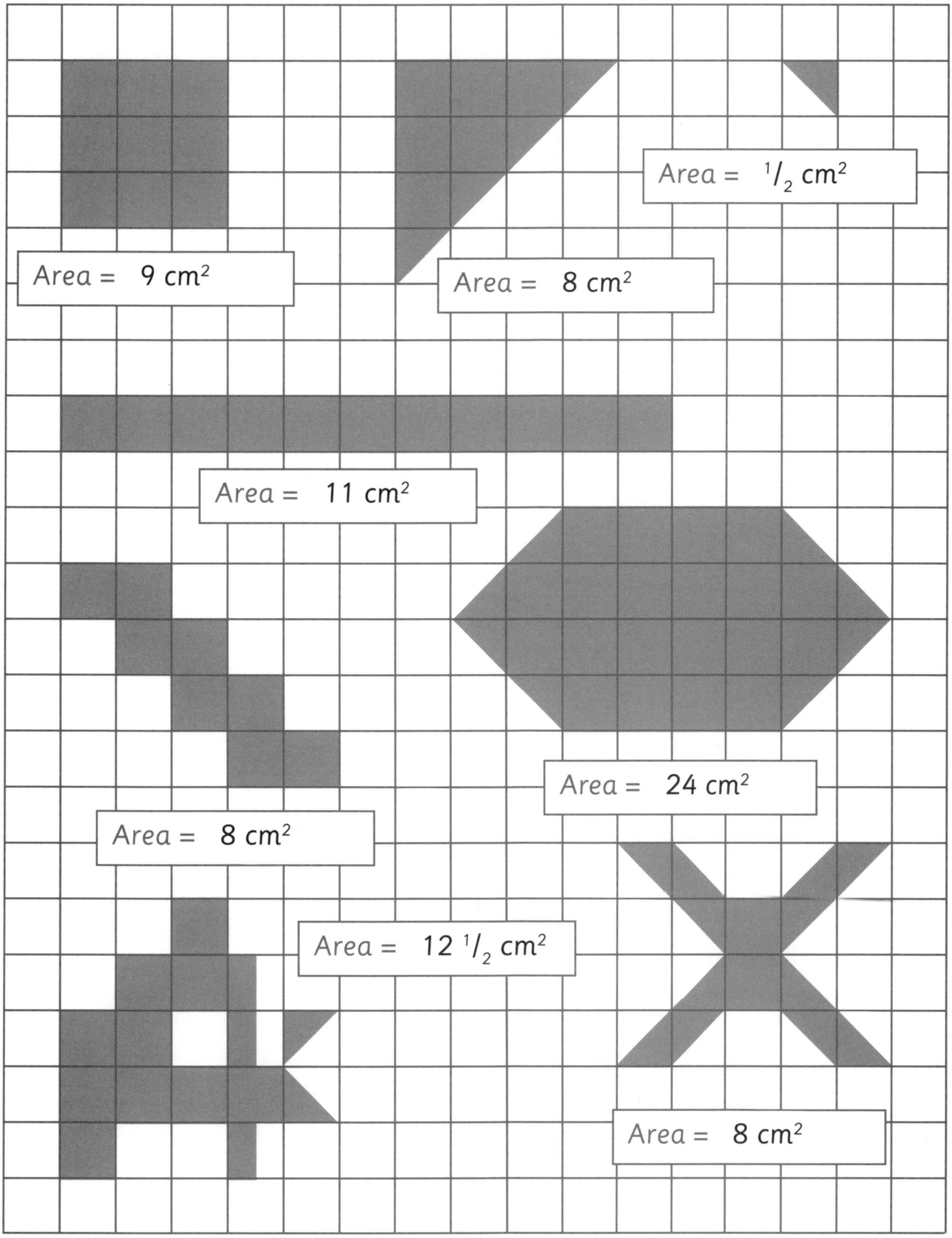

Name: Date:

More Area

On the grid, draw as many shapes as you can which have an area of 8 cm^2.

You can use whole squares and half squares.

Homework Today Answer Sheet

Number 16

Name: Date:

More Area

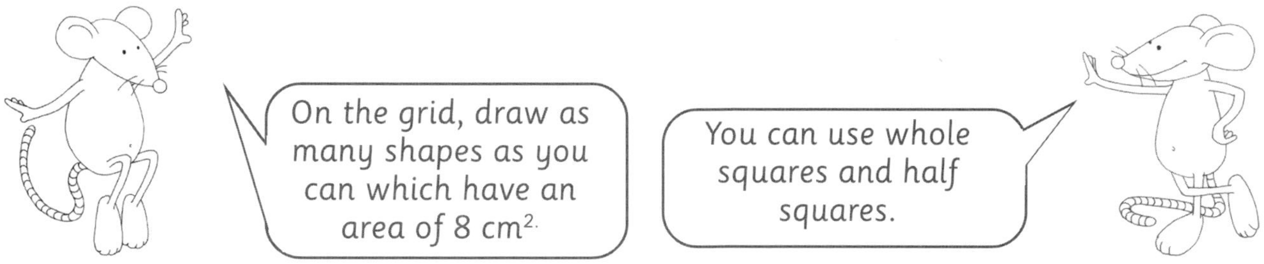

The answers to this page will be created by the individual pupil.

Homework Today

Name: Date:

Centuries

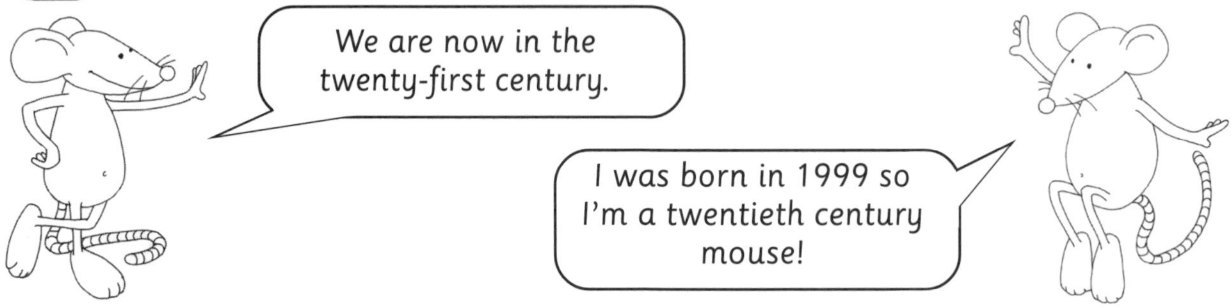

These dates all start with 19 but we say that they were in the twentieth century:

1901 1914 1939 1955

These dates all start with 10 but we say that they were in the eleventh century:

1066 1088 1099

Roman armies left Britain in the year 407.
We say that this was in the fifth century.

Look at each date below. Write in words what century it was in.
Be careful with your spellings.

1945 →		1812 →	
1588 →		1606 →	
1189 →		729 →	
1066 →		62 →	
1214 →		1778 →	
1352 →		814 →	

What famous event took place in 1066?

Homework Today Answer Sheet

Number 17

Name: Date:

Centuries

We are now in the twenty-first century.

I was born in 1999 so I'm a twentieth century mouse!

These dates all start with 19 but we say that they were in the twentieth century:

1901 1914 1939 1955

These dates all start with 10 but we say that they were in the eleventh century:

1066 1088 1099

Roman armies left Britain in the year 407.
We say that this was in the fifth century.

Look at each date below. Write in words what century it was in.
Be careful with your spellings.

1945 →	twentieth century	1812 →	nineteenth century
1588 →	sixteenth century	1606 →	seventeenth century
1189 →	twelfth century	729 →	eighth century
1066 →	eleventh century	62 →	first century
1214 →	thirteenth century	1778 →	eighteenth century
1352 →	fourteenth century	814 →	ninth century

What famous event took place in 1066?

The Battle of Hastings

Number 18

Homework Today

Name: Date:

Months of the Year

Use your best handwriting to copy this rhyme.

Thirty days has September,
April, June and November.
All the rest have thirty-one,
exccept for February alone,
which has twenty-eight days clear
and twenty-nine in each leap year.

Now use the rhyme to help you to state the number of days in each month.

January	→	☐			
February	→	☐	or	☐	in a leap year
March	→	☐	August	→	☐
April	→	☐	September	→	☐
May	→	☐	October	→	☐
June	→	☐	November	→	☐
July	→	☐	December	→	☐

Homework Today — Answer Sheet

Number **18**

Name: Date:

Months of the Year

Use your best handwriting to copy this rhyme.

Thirty days has September,
April, June and November.
All the rest have thirty-one,
except for February alone,
which has twenty-eight days clear
and twenty-nine in each leap year.

Now use the rhyme to help you to state the number of days in each month.

January	→	31				
February	→	28	or	29	in a leap year	
March	→	31		August	→	31
April	→	30		September	→	30
May	→	31		October	→	31
June	→	30		November	→	30
July	→	31		December	→	31

Number 19

Homework Today

Name: Date:

Minutes, Hours and Days

There are sixty minutes in an hour.

How many minutes are there in two hours? ☐

How many minutes are there in three hours? ☐

How many minutes are there in half an hour? ☐

How many minutes are there in a quarter of an hour? ☐

How many minutes in:

$1\frac{1}{2}$ hours? ☐ $2\frac{1}{2}$ hours? ☐ $1\frac{1}{4}$ hours? ☐

There are twenty-four hours in a day.

How many hours are there in two days? ☐

How many hours are there in three days? ☐

How many hours are there in four days? ☐

Can you work out the number of hours in a week? ☐

How many hours are there in half a day? ☐

If you want to, try to work out how many minutes there are in one day.

☐

Homework Today Answer Sheet

Number 19

Name: Date:

Minutes, Hours and Days

There are sixty minutes in an hour.

How many minutes are there in two hours? 120

How many minutes are there in three hours? 180

How many minutes are there in half an hour? 30

How many minutes are there in a quarter of an hour? 15

How many minutes in:

$1\frac{1}{2}$ hours? 90 $2\frac{1}{2}$ hours? 150 $1\frac{1}{4}$ hours? 75

There are twenty-four hours in a day.

How many hours are there in two days? 48

How many hours are there in three days? 72

How many hours are there in four days? 96

Can you work out the number of hours in a week? 168

How many hours are there in half a day? 12

If you want to, try to work out how many minutes there are in one day.

1440

Number

20

Homework Today

Name: Date:

A Bar-chart

This bar-chart shows the number of books borrowed from the library each school day last week.

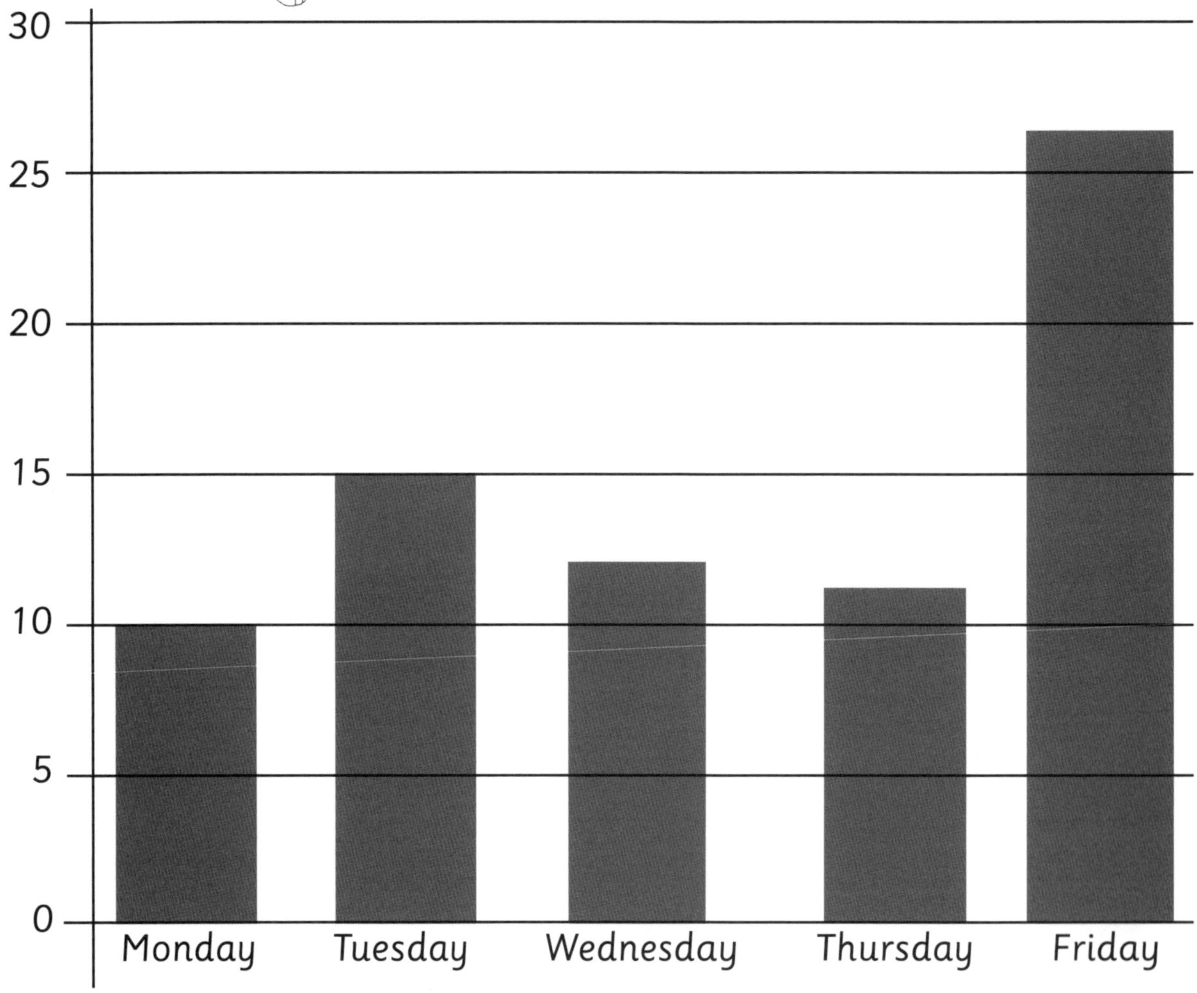

Roughly how many books were borrowed each day?

Monday [ ] Tuesday [ ] Wednesday [ ]

Thursday [ ] Friday [ ]

Roughly how many books were borrowed altogether? [ ]

Can you think of a reason why more books were borrowed on Friday than on any other day?

____

____

Homework Today Answer Sheet

Number 20

Name: Date:

A Bar-chart

This bar-chart shows the number of books borrowed from the library each school day last week.

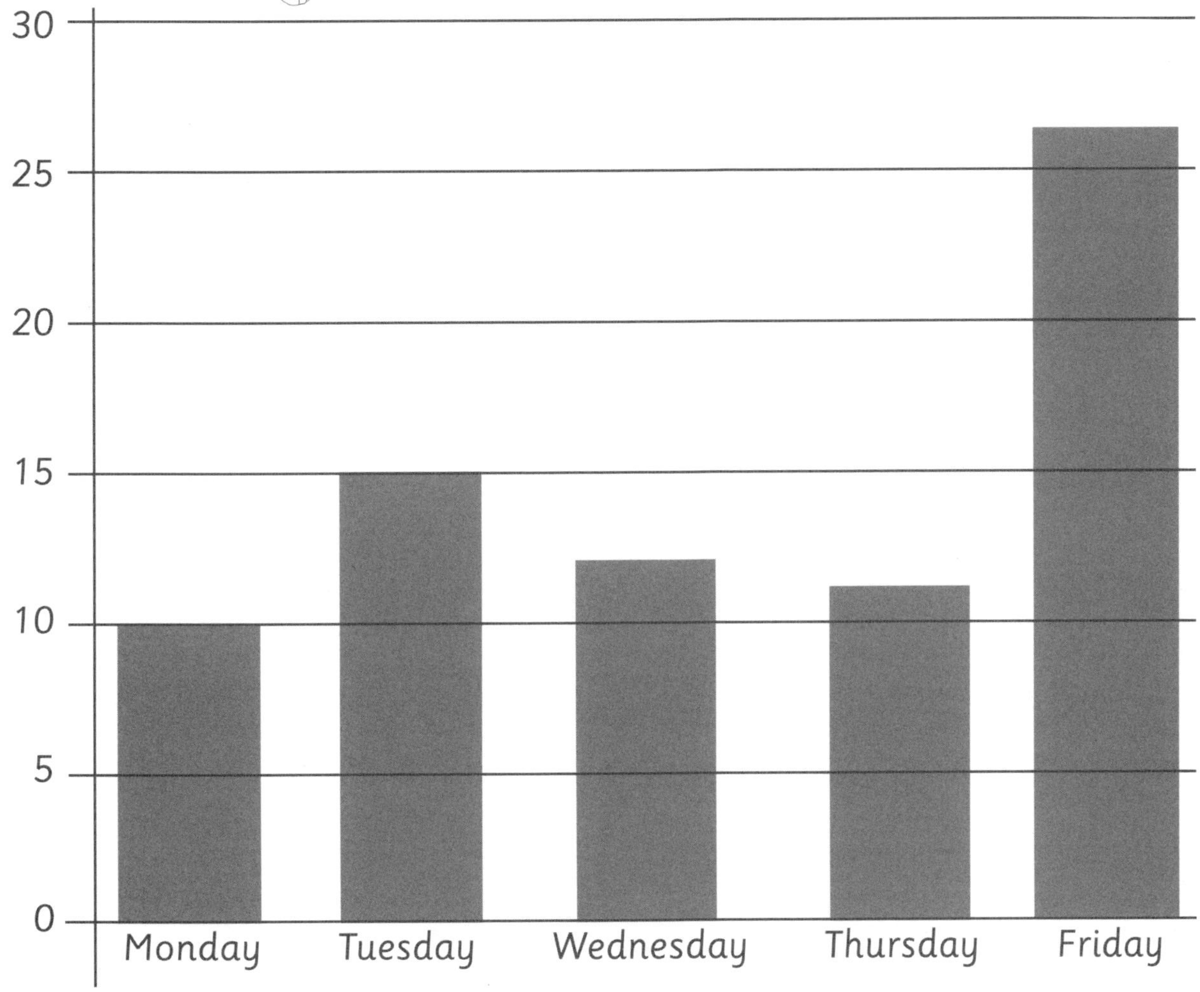

Roughly how many books were borrowed each day?

Monday 10 Tuesday 15 Wednesday 12

Thursday 11 Friday 26

Roughly how many books were borrowed altogether? 74

Can you think of a reason why more books were borrowed on Friday than on any other day?

Pupils took out books for reading on Friday for use over the weekend when they had more free time.

Number

21

Homework Today

Name: Date:

Rhyming Couplets

A rhyming couplet is two lines with rhyming words at the end of each.

Complete this poem by writing the second line of each couplet; the first two couplets have been done for you.

A, B, C,
Time for tea.

D, E, F,
My friend Jeff.

G, H, I,
____

J, K, L,
____

M, N, O,
____

P, Q, R,
____

S, T, U,,
____

V, W,
____

X, Y, Z,
____

Read your poem aloud to a friend.

Homework Today Answer Sheet

Number 21

Name: Date:

Rhyming Couplets

Complete this poem by writing the second line of each couplet; the first two couplets have been done for you.

A, B, C,
Time for tea.

D, E, F,
My friend Jeff.

G, H, I,
Eat some pie.

J, K, L,
Can you spell?

M, N, O,
It's time to go.

P, Q, R,
A chocolate bar.

S, T, U,,
Let's eat stew.

V, W,
Get in the queue.

X, Y, Z,
Time for bed.

These are sample answers. The children will have many other successful ideas.

Number 22

Homework Today

Name: Date:

Alliteration

Alliteration is often found in poetry. It uses words that begin with the same sound.

Complete this alliteration alphabet. The first two letters have been done for you.

A = Alligators and ants are often annoying.

B = Bouncing bananas sometimes bring bluebottles.

C = ______

D = ______

E = ______

F = ______

G = ______

H = ______

I = ______

J = ______

K = ______

L = ______

M = ______

N = ______

O = ______

P = ______

Q = ______

R = ______

S = ______

T = ______

U = ______

V = ______

W = ______

X = ______

Y = ______

Z = ______

Homework Today Answer Sheet

Number
22

Name: Date:

Alliteration

Alliteration is often found in poetry. It uses words that begin with the same sound.

Complete this alliteration alphabet. The first two letters have been done for you.

A = Alligators and ants are often annoying.
B = Bouncing bananas sometimes bring bluebottles.
C = Clever cats catch cockroaches with their claws.
D = Dizzy ducks dance delightfully.
E = Elephants eat enormous eggs.
F = Funny frogs fly over France.
G = Groovy great granny grabs grapes.
H = Happy hyenas hope for hats.
I = Ice includes irresistible icicles.
J = Jumping jaguars juggle jelly.
K = Kimberley kangaroo kicked a koala.
L = Lucy the lollipop lady loves lemons.
M = Mister Mouse is married to Mrs Mouse.
N = Naughty Nathan nags nanny nervously.
O = Olly Octopus owned oranges.
P = Peggy picked a peppermint.
Q = Quiet queen quickly questioned.
R = Ragged Robin ripped a ribbon.
S = Silly Simon slipped in the street.
T = Tiny tortoise treasures his teddy.
U = Upset unicorns are under umbrellas.
V = Violent Vicky makes vases.
W = Wild wolves want wicked weasels.
X = Xenon had an excellent x-ray.
Y = Yummy yellow yoghurts.
Z = Zany zebra zig-zagged.

These are just examples of the sort of answers that may be done by year 4 children.

Number 23

Homework Today

Name: Date:

Alphabetical Order

Arrange these groups of words into alphabetical order. You may need to look at the third, fourth and fifth letters with care to be sure to get it right.

string stretch stripe struggle stick street stop
stab still strain strap stitch

1.____ 4.____ 7.____ 10.____
2.____ 5.____ 8.____ 11.____
3.____ 6.____ 9.____ 12.____

banana basket banter back banger badger
badminton bandstand bamboo bank bargain barber

1.____ 4.____ 7.____ 10.____
2.____ 5.____ 8.____ 11.____
3.____ 6.____ 9.____ 12.____

fraction free France front fruit fringe frost
frame fry frill fresh froth

1.____ 4.____ 7.____ 10.____
2.____ 5.____ 8.____ 11.____
3.____ 6.____ 9.____ 12.____

Homework Today Answer Sheet

Number 23

Name: Date:

Alphabetical Order

Arrange these groups of words into alphabetical order. You may need to look at the third, fourth and fifth letters with care to be sure to get it right.

string stretch stripe struggle stick street stop stab still strain strap stitch

1. stab	4. stitch	7. strap	10. string
2. stick	5. stop	8. street	11. stripe
3. still	6. strain	9. stretch	12. struggle

banana basket banter back banger badger badminton bandstand bamboo bank bargain barber

1. back	4. bamboo	7. banger	10. barber
2. badger	5. banana	8. bank	11. bargain
3. badminton	6. bandstand	9. banter	12. basket

fraction free France front fruit fringe frost frame fry frill fresh froth

1. fraction	4. free	7. fringe	10. froth
2. frame	5. fresh	8. front	11. fruit
3. France	6. frill	9. frost	12. fry

Number 24

Homework Today

Name: Date:

Double Consonants

Look at the words in the word bank below. What do you notice about them?

Suffolk	butter	saddle	kettle	muddle
bubbles	mittens	kitten	suffix	middle

Did you notice that they all have two syllables and they all have a double consonant in them?

Put the words from the word bank, into the sentences below.

1. The children enjoyed blowing ______________.
2. The mother cat watched her ______________ playing.
3. You can boil water in a ______________.
4. I like peanut ______________ in my sandwiches.
5. He was in the ______________ of the crowd.
6. She got in a dreadful ______________ with her homework.
7. The ______________ was put on the horse.
8. A ______________ goes at the end of a word.
9. ______________ is a county in the east of England.

Can you think of at least ten more double consonant words?
Write them on the back of the sheet.

Homework Today — Answer Sheet

Number 24

Name: Date:

Double Consonants

Look at the words in the word bank below. What do you notice about them?

Suffolk	butter	saddle	kettle	muddle
bubbles	mittens	kitten	suffix	middle

Did you notice that they all have two syllables and they all have a double consonant in them?

Put the words from the word bank, into the sentences below.

1. The children enjoyed blowing __bubbles__.
2. The mother cat watched her __kitten__ playing.
3. You can boil water in a __kettle__.
4. I like peanut __butter__ in my sandwiches.
5. He was in the __middle__ of the crowd.
6. She got in a dreadful __muddle__ with her homework.
7. The __saddle__ was put on the horse.
8. A __suffix__ goes at the end of a word.
9. __Suffolk__ is a county in the east of England.

Can you think of at least ten more double consonant words?
Write them on the back of the sheet.

Number 25

Homework Today

Name: Date:

More Rhyming Couplets

Two lines with rhyming words at the end of each,
is called a rhyming couplet.

Here is my favourite rhyming couplet.
'I was being chased by a very fierce cat,
When along came a dog and squashed him flat!'

rock	road	three	fall	wall	heard
	toad	tree	clock	bird	

Choose words from the word bank to complete these couplets.

1. I was driving along the ________________,
   When I suddenly saw a large green ________________.

2. In the field there grew a ________________,
   Apples grew on it, one, two ________________.

3. Tick, tock goes the grandfather ________________,
   When it chimes, the house will ________________.

4. Climbing up to the top of the ________________,
   "Oh dear!" he yelled as he started to ________________.

5. I listened carefully, and I ________________,
   The singing of a little ________________.

On the back of this sheet, make up two rhyming couplets of your own.

Homework Today   Answer Sheet

Number 25

Name: Date:

More Rhyming Couplets

Two lines with rhyming words at the end of each,
is called a rhyming couplet.

Here is my favourite rhyming couplet.
'I was being chased by a very fierce cat,
When along came a dog and squashed him flat!'

rock	road	three	fall	wall	heard
	toad	tree	clock	bird	

Choose words from the word bank to complete these couplets.

1. I was driving along the road,
   When I suddenly saw a large green toad.

2. In the field there grew a tree,
   Apples grew on it, one, two three.

3. Tick, tock goes the grandfather clock,
   When it chimes, the house will rock.

4. Climbing up to the top of the wall,
   "Oh dear!" he yelled as he started to fall.

5. I listened carefully, and I heard,
   The singing of a little bird.

On the back of this sheet, make up two rhyming couplets of your own

Number

26

Homework Today

Name: Date:

Nouns, Adjectives and Verbs

Complete the passage below by putting interesting adjectives in the spaces.

It was a ______________ August day. The sun sparkled on the ______________ sea and the laughter of ______________ children could be heard on the beach. Corrine and Sanjay enjoyed building a castle near the water's edge. They worked hard to make it as large as possible, putting ______________ towers on it and decorating it with carefully collected seashells and ______________ paper flags.

Use the boxes below to write down all the nouns and verbs you can find in the writing.

Nouns	Verbs

Homework Today Answer Sheet

Number 26

Name: Date:

Nouns, Adjectives and Verbs

Complete the passage below by putting interesting adjectives in the spaces.

It was a brilliant August day. The sun sparkled on the warm sea and the laughter of happy children could be heard on the beach. Corrine and Sanjay enjoyed building a castle near the water's edge. They worked hard to make it as large as possible, putting square towers on it and decorating it with carefully collected seashells and colourful paper flags.

These are just a few of the many possible adjectives that could be used.

Use the boxes below to write down all the nouns and verbs you can find in the writing.

Nouns	Verbs
day sun sea laughter children beach castle water edge towers seashells paper flags	was sparkled heard enjoyed collected building worked make putting decorating

Number

27

Homework Today

Name: Date:

Adverbs

An adverb shows how a verb might be done.
Choose three adverbs from the box below that might be used to describe each of the verbs. You can use words more than once.

happily	fearfully	angrily	noisily	loudly	
quietly	crossly	unsteadily	excitedly	slowly	clearly

1. The man walked

2. The children played

3. She yelled

4. The old lady spoke

Did you notice that the adverbs all had the 'ly' suffix?
On the back of this sheet write down four more 'ly' adverbs.

Homework Today Answer Sheet

Number 27

Name: Date:

Adverbs

An adverb shows how a verb might be done.
Choose three adverbs from the box below that might be used to describe each of the verbs. You can use words more than once.

happily	fearfully	angrily	noisily	loudly	
quietly	crossly	unsteadily	excitedly	slowly	clearly

1. The man walked — unsteadily / quickly / slowly

2. The children played — noisily / happily / excitedly

These are possible answers; variations are acceptable.

3. She yelled — crossly / angrily / loudly

4. The old lady spoke — quietly / clearly / fearfully

On the back of this sheet write down four more 'ly' adverbs.
There are many possibilities. One could use: CLUMSILY, STRANGELY, HEAVILY, LIGHTLY

Number 28

Homework Today

Name: Date:

Alphabetical Animals

This alphabet may help you to arrange the animals in the box into alphabetical order.

lion	leopard	panther	cheetah	jaguar	fox
cat	mouse	hamster	gerbil	sheep	cow
pig	goat	llama	ferret	kangaroo	wombat
wallaby	lizard	alpaca	monkey	rat	moose
boar	buffalo	anteater	iguana	wolf	camel
armadillo	rabbit	chimpanzee	gorilla	squirrel	
hedgehog	weasel	yak	hare	walrus	

1. ______	11. ______	21. ______	31. ______
2. ______	12. ______	22. ______	32. ______
3. ______	13. ______	23. ______	33. ______
4. ______	14. ______	24. ______	34. ______
5. ______	15. ______	25. ______	35. ______
6. ______	16. ______	26. ______	36. ______
7. ______	17. ______	27. ______	37. ______
8. ______	18. ______	28. ______	38. ______
9. ______	19. ______	29. ______	39. ______
10. ______	20. ______	30. ______	40. ______

A B C D E F G H I J K L M N O P Q R S T U V W X Y Z

Now check to make sure that you have copied the spelling for each animal correctly.

Homework Today Answer Sheet

Number 28

Name: Date:

Alphabetical Animals

This alphabet may help you to arrange the animals in the box into alphabetical order.

A B C D E F G H I J K L M N O P Q R S T U V W X Y Z

lion	leopard	panther	cheetah	jaguar	fox
cat	mouse	hamster	gerbil	sheep	cow
pig	goat	llama	ferret	kangaroo	wombat
wallaby	lizard	alpaca	monkey	rat	moose
boar	buffalo	anteater	iguana	wolf	camel
armadillo	rabbit	chimpanzee	gorilla	squirrel	
hedgehog	weasel	yak	hare	walrus	

1. alpaca	11. ferret	21. kangaroo	31. rabbit
2. anteater	12. fox	22. leopard	32. rat
3. armadillo	13. gerbil	23. lion	33. sheep
4. boar	14. goat	24. lizard	34. squirrel
5. buffalo	15. gorilla	25. llama	35. wallaby
6. camel	16. hamster	26. monkey	36. walrus
7. cat	17. hare	27. moose	37. weasel
8. cheetah	18. hedgehog	28. mouse	38. wolf
9. chimpanzee	19. iguana	29. panther	39. wombat
10. cow	20. jaguar	30. pig	40. yak

Now check to make sure that you have copied the spelling for each animal correctly.

Homework Today

Name: Date:

Gender Words

1.

duck	queen
girl	bull
king	vixen
fox	boy
cow	drake

2.

male	man
doe	female
woman	ewe
goose	buck
ram	gander

3.

prince	empress
tiger	lioness
duke	tigress
emperor	princess
lion	duchess

What do you notice about all the 'female' words in set 3?

____

____

Can you think of some more pairs of gender words to write?

male	female

male	female

Homework Today	**Answer Sheet**	Number 29

Name: Date:

Gender Words

Match up the pairs of words that tell us if something is male or female.

1.

duck	queen
girl	bull
king	vixen
fox	boy
cow	drake

2.

male	man
doe	female
woman	ewe
goose	buck
ram	gander

3.

prince	empress
tiger	lioness
duke	tigress
emperor	princess
lion	duchess

What do you notice about all the 'female' words in set 3?

They all end in 'ess'.

Can you think of some more pairs of gender words to write?
These are just a few of the possible answers.

male	female
cockerel	hen
earl	countess
father	mother

male	female
billy-goat	nanny-goat
stallion	mare
uncle	aunt

Number

30

Homework Today

Name: Date:

Comparative Adjectives

These adjectives describe different levels of things.

Match each group of adjectives to a subject they might describe.

good	better	best		film
bad	worse	worst		tortoise
cool	warm	hot		wrestler
fast	faster	fastest		comedian
slow	slower	slowest		behaviour
strong	stronger	strongest		water
funny	funnier	funniest		athlete

Now find the sets of adjectives, from the box ,in the word search below.

light medium dark strange stranger
strangest cool cold freezing close closer
closest new old ancient

T	S	V	R	R	T	O	O	L	D	G	L	I	G	H	T	G	C	H	V	X
J	O	F	T	E	N	F	T	R	S	L	J	U	L	I	C	O	L	D	O	Z
E	M	T	S	V	R	O	X	E	F	S	O	O	S	E	L	R	R	T	J	U
K	E	L	E	L	F	T	S	S	R	T	T	R	C	L	O	S	E	R	B	O
H	T	U	U	N	C	L	O	S	E	X	R	L	E	N	S	T	K	V	L	T
L	I	Z	M	E	D	I	U	M	E	C	A	K	E	S	E	N	D	A	R	K
F	M	O	P	S	T	I	L	T	Z	V	A	V	E	F	S	H	I	K	M	O
N	E	V	E	R	A	B	C	D	I	S	H	Y	G	S	T	R	A	N	G	E
S	S	B	E	R	D	C	R	A	N	E	W	X	B	B	R	L	J	L	E	N
W	R	N	A	N	C	O	U	L	G	V	I	R	M	I	S	Z	T	R	O	Y
V	S	T	R	A	N	G	E	R	E	R	T	S	D	A	N	C	I	E	N	T
H	D	S	T	R	I	S	S	M	A	B	C	O	A	E	S	T	R	L	O	L
L	O	S	O	O	C	O	O	L	E	B	R	S	T	R	A	N	G	E	S	T

Homework Today Answer Sheet

Number 30

Name: Date:

Comparative Adjectives

Match each group of adjectives to a subject they might describe.

			Subject (as printed)	Answer (lines drawn)
good	better	best	film	film / behaviour
bad	worse	worst	tortoise	film / behaviour
cool	warm	hot	wrestler	water
fast	faster	fastest	comedian	athlete
slow	slower	slowest	behaviour	tortoise
strong	stronger	strongest	water	wrestler
funny	funnier	funniest	athlete	comedian

Other alternatives are acceptable.

Now find the sets of adjectives, from the box ,in the word search below.

light medium dark strange stranger
strangest cool cold freezing close closer
closest new old ancient

T	S	V	R	R	T	O	O	L	D	G	L	I	G	H	T	G	C	H	V	X
J	O	F	T	E	N	F	T	R	S	L	J	U	L	I	C	O	L	D	O	Z
E	M	T	S	V	R	O	X	E	F	S	O	O	S	E	L	R	R	T	J	U
K	E	L	E	L	F	T	S	S	R	T	T	R	C	L	O	S	E	R	B	O
H	T	U	U	N	C	L	O	S	E	X	R	L	E	N	S	T	K	V	L	T
L	I	Z	M	E	D	I	U	M	E	C	A	K	E	S	E	N	D	A	R	K
F	M	O	P	S	T	I	L	T	Z	V	A	V	E	F	S	H	I	K	M	O
N	E	V	E	R	A	B	C	D	I	S	H	Y	G	S	T	R	A	N	G	E
S	S	B	E	R	D	C	R	A	N	E	W	X	B	B	R	L	J	L	E	N
W	R	N	A	N	C	O	U	L	G	V	I	R	M	I	S	Z	T	R	O	Y
V	S	T	R	A	N	G	E	R	E	R	T	S	D	A	N	C	I	E	N	T
H	D	S	T	R	I	S	S	M	A	B	C	O	A	E	S	T	R	L	O	L
L	O	S	O	O	C	O	O	L	E	B	R	S	T	R	A	N	G	E	S	T

Number 31

Homework Today

Name: Date:

Building a Character

Invent a character by answering the questions below.

Is the person male or female? ______

What is his/her name? ______

Is she/he young, middle aged or old? ______

Where does he/she live? ______

Who does he/she live with? ______

Does he/she have a job? What is it? ______

Describe his/her:

a) Hair colour and style. ______

b) Face. ______

c) Height. ______

d) Build. ______

Is she/he: cheerful? ______ miserable? ______

fussy? ______ moody? ______

Now write an interesting paragraph describing your character. You may add any information you wish to, to help your reader to get to know your character. Turn over the sheet and carry on if you run out of space.

______

______

______

______

______

______

______

Homework Today **Answer Sheet**

Number 31

Name: Date:

Building a Character

Invent a character by answering the questions below.

Is the person male or female? ____________

What is his/her name? ____________

Is she/he young, middle aged or old? ____________

Where does he/she live? ____________

Who does he/she live with? ____________

Does he/she have a job? What is it? ____________

Describe his/her:

a) Hair colour and style. ____________

b) Face. ____________

c) Height. ____________

d) Build. ____________

Is she/he: cheerful? ____________ miserable? ____________

fussy? ____________ moody? ____________

Now write an interesting paragraph describing your character. You may add any information you wish to, to help your reader to get to know your character. Turn over the sheet and carry on if you run out of space.

The responses to the above questions and also the content of the paragraph will be individual to each pupil.

Number 32

Homework Today

Name: Date:

Describing a Character

Write a paragraph describing a dog. Make your description as detailed as possible and try to include at least three words that you have not used before in your writing. Use the words in the word bank to help you.

fierce snarling bumbling gentle menacing
powerful grotesque growl slobbery playful inquisitive
shaggy disposition temperament furry miniature
boisterous bouncy courageous amiable yapping
curly faithful energetic

Underline any words that you have never used before in your writing. Are there at least three? Well done!

Homework Today — Answer Sheet

Number 32

Name: Date:

Describing a Character

Write a paragraph describing a dog. Make your description as detailed as possible and try to include at least three words that you have not used before in your writing. Use the words in the word bank to help you.

fierce snarling bumbling gentle menacing powerful grotesque growl slobbery playful inquisitive shaggy disposition temperament furry miniature boisterous bouncy courageous amiable yapping curly faithful energetic

<u>The content of this paragraph will be individual to the pupil.</u>

Underline any words that you have never used before in your writing. Are there at least three? Well done!

Number 33

Homework Today

Name: Date:

Turning Notes into Prose

Read these notes about a school trip to the zoo.

Coach left 9.15 am.
Arrived zoo 10.30 am.
Pupils in groups of six.
All types of animals, reptiles etc. seen.
Saw seals fed 1.00 pm.
Visited zoo gift shop.
Departed 3.00 pm.
Returned to school 4.15 pm.

Now turn these notes about the zoo trip, into an interesting article suitable for publication in the school magazine or newsletter. You may choose to write about it as if you were on the trip.

Homework Today — Answer Sheet

Number 33

Name: Date:

Turning Notes into Prose

Read these notes about a school trip to the zoo.

Coach left 9.15 am.
Arrived zoo 10.30 am.
Pupils in groups of six.
All types of animals, reptiles etc. seen.
Saw seals fed 1.00 pm.
Visited zoo gift shop.
Departed 3.00 pm.
Returned to school 4.15 pm.

Now turn these notes about the zoo trip, into an interesting article suitable for publication in the school magazine or newsletter. You may choose to write about it as if you were on the trip.

Sample Answer

A coach full of excited children looking forward to visiting the zoo, left school at 9.15 am and reached its destination after an hour and a quarter.

The zoo had a range of different creatures from many countries. The pupils toured the zoo in groups of six, and then met up at one o'clock to enjoy seeing the seals fed. After an interesting day that also included camel rides and of course an opportunity to visit the gift shop, it was time to leave.

A coach full of tired children left the zoo at 3.00 pm and arrived back at school at 4.15 pm.

Number 34

Homework Today

Name: Date:

Technical Vocabulary

Answer the clues to complete the crossword using the words in the box.

prefix synonym suffix homophone monologue vowel antonym simile noun adverb adjective syllable plural consonant paragraph singular illustration fiction prefix glossary verb punctuation pronoun alliteration

Clues across
1. A word with the same meaning as another word.
4. Letters in front of a word.
6. A word that sounds the same as another word but has a different meaning (eg: pair, pear).
7. A word used in place of a noun (eg: he, it, they).
9. A naming word.
11. A list of words and their meanings - often at the back of a book.
13. A picture in a book.
14. A word showing how a verb is done (eg: quickly).
16. Not a vowel.
18. One of the distinct sounds in a word.
19. A word meaning the opposite to another word.
20. A describing word.

Clues down
1. A word ending.
2. A way of describing something as like something else (eg: as old as the hills).
3. Only one.
4. Marks used to help you to understand writing (eg: comma).
5. A long speech, spoken by one person.
7. A new section of a piece of writing.
8. A phrase with words starting with the same letter.
10. An invented story.
12. A, E, I, O or U.
15. A doing word.
17. More than one.

Homework Today Answer Sheet

Number 34

Name: Date:

Technical Vocabulary

Answer the clues to complete the crossword using the words in the box.

prefix synonym suffix homophone monologue vowel antonym simile noun adverb adjective syllable plural consonant paragraph singular illustration fiction prefix glossary verb punctuation pronoun alliteration

Clues across
1. A word with the same meaning as another word.
4. Letters in front of a word.
6. A word that sounds the same as another word but has a different meaning (eg: pair, pear).
7. A word used in place of a noun (eg: he, it, they).
9. A naming word.
11. A list of words and their meanings - often at the back of a book.
13. A picture in a book.
14. A word showing how a verb is done (eg: quickly).
16. Not a vowel.
18. One of the distinct sounds in a word.
19. A word meaning the opposite to another word.
20. A describing word.

Clues down
1. A word ending.
2. A way of describing something as like something else (eg: as old as the hills).
3. Only one.
4. Marks used to help you to understand writing (eg: comma).
5. A long speech, spoken by one person.
7. A new section of a piece of writing.
8. A phrase with words starting with the same letter.
10. An invented story.
12. A, E, I, O or U.
15. A doing word.
17. More than one.

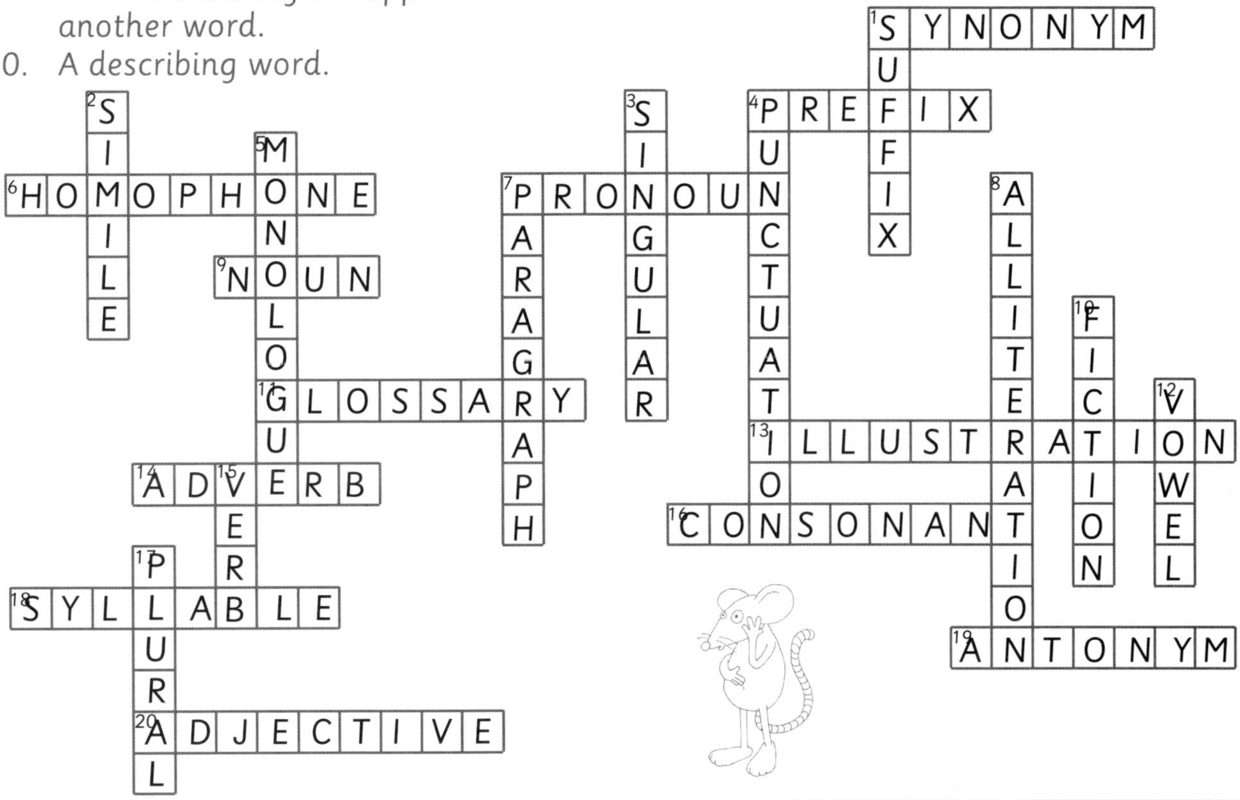

Name: Date:

Pyramid Puzzle

Answer the clues using the words in the box to help you complete my pyramid puzzle.

1. Sun God.
2. Sky Goddess.
3. River running through Egypt.
4. Country of pyramids and pharaohs.
5. Stone statue with lion's body and man's head.
6. In the far distant past.
7. Egyptian rulers.
8. Stone tablet for writing.
9. Famous young pharaoh.
10. Alphabet made from picture symbols.

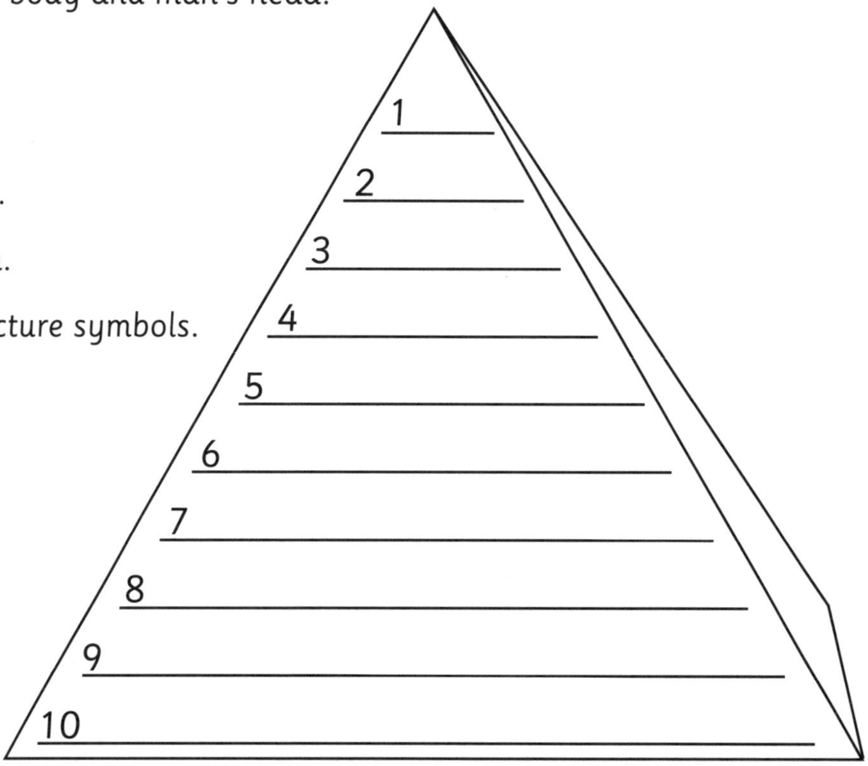

Ra Pharaohs
Tutankhamen
Cartouche Nut
Egypt Nile
Ancient Sphinx
Hieroglyphics

Now write four interesting facts about ancient Egypt.

1. ____________________

2. ____________________

3. ____________________

4. ____________________

Homework Today Answer Sheet

Number 35

Name: Date:

Pyramid Puzzle

Answer the clues using the words in the box to help you complete my pyramid puzzle.

1. Sun God.
2. Sky Goddess.
3. River running through Egypt.
4. Country of pyramids and pharaohs.
5. Stone statue with lion's body and man's head.
6. In the far distant past.
7. Egyptian rulers.
8. Stone tablet for writing.
9. Famous young pharaoh.
10. Alphabet made from picture symbols.

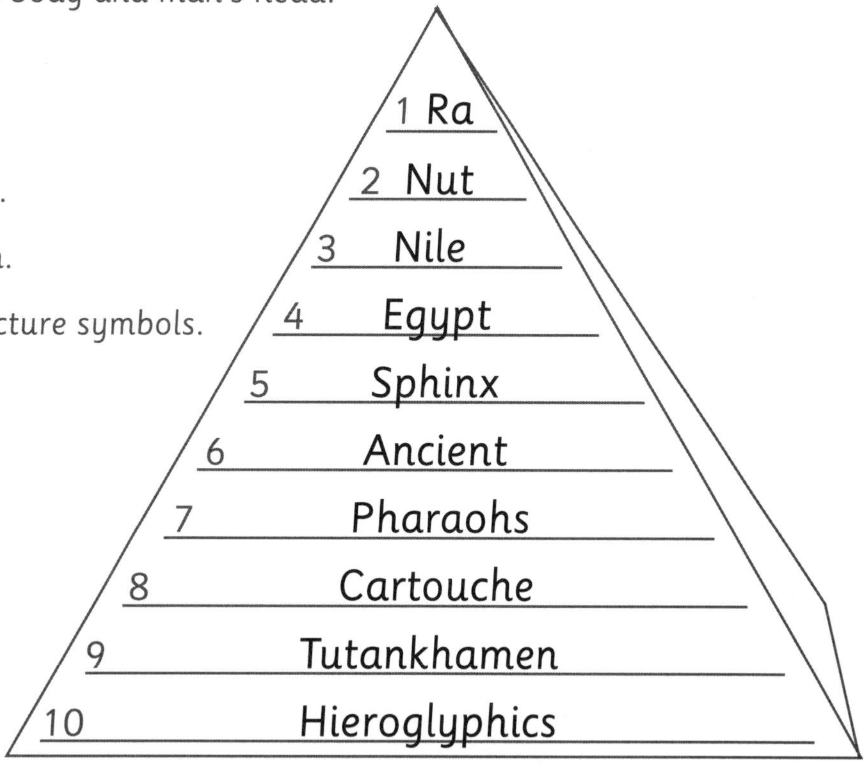

Ra Pharaohs
Tutankhamen
Cartouche Nut
Egypt Nile
Ancient Sphinx
Hieroglyphics

Now write four interesting facts about ancient Egypt.

1.
2. After learning about ancient Egypt, the answers to this
3. section will be many and varied. These would be
4. excellent for a class 'sharing' session.

Number 36

Homework Today

Name: Date:

Now and Then

Look at the pictures below. Beside them write about what is similar to today and what is different from today.

Similar to today	Different from today

Homework Today Answer Sheet

Number 36

Name: Date:

Now and Then

Look at the pictures below. Beside them write about what is similar to today and what is different from today.

Possible answers

Similar to today	Different from today
Children today play on bicycles. Bicycles can look similar and be made from same types of materials. Girl's shoes look like shoes of today.	Girl's hairstyle. Children's style of clothing. Basket on front of bicycle. 'Black and white' photos may be mentioned.

Similar to today	Different from today
Plain painted walls.	Shape of mirror. Design of fireplace. Woman wearing apron.

Open fire and grandfather clock is valid in both sections depending on the pupils' experiences.

Number 37

Homework Today

Name: Date:

Turning Prose into Notes

Read the story extract below, with care.

Mrs Richards went into the police station looking very worried. She approached the sergeant on the front desk.
"Can I help you madam?" he asked.
"It's dreadful, my daughter Ella is missing," came the unhappy reply. "We were all on the beach near the pier where she was playing happily. I looked in the other direction for a few moments and when I looked back again she had vanished."
"I need to take her details so that we can organise a search for her," said the sergeant. "Tell me your daughter's age and describe her for me."
"Ella is nine years old, quite tall for her age and usually quite cheerful and chatty. She has lovely brown eyes and longish dark wavy hair that she likes to pull back into a ponytail."
"What was she wearing?"
"Well of course I made her wear her sweatshirt when we left home, but she took that off as soon as we reached the beach. So now she is wearing her bright green flowery t-shirt, her favourite orange shorts and a pair of white sandals. I'm so worried. Whatever can have happened to her?" sobbed Mrs Richards.
"I'm sure we will find her soon, Mrs Richards," said the sergeant reassuringly. "Your excellent description will help us."

Now see if you can pick out the useful information, and write notes that will help the police to find Ella.

____

____

____

____

____

____

____

You will be pleased to know that Ella was spotted a short time later. She was by the ice-cream van, where she had wandered off to buy a lolly. The police told her to make sure an adult always knew where she was in future.

Homework Today Answer Sheet

Number **37**

Name: Date:

Turning Prose into Notes

Read the story extract below, with care.

Mrs Richards went into the police station looking very worried. She approached the sergeant on the front desk.
"Can I help you madam?" he asked.
"It's dreadful, my daughter Ella is missing," came the unhappy reply. "We were all on the beach near the pier where she was playing happily. I looked in the other direction for a few moments and when I looked back again she had vanished."
"I need to take her details so that we can organise a search for her," said the sergeant. "Tell me your daughter's age and describe her for me."
"Ella is nine years old, quite tall for her age and usually quite cheerful and chatty. She has lovely brown eyes and longish dark wavy hair that she likes to pull back into a ponytail."
"What was she wearing?"
"Well of course I made her wear her sweatshirt when we left home, but she took that off as soon as we reached the beach. So now she is wearing her bright green flowery t-shirt, her favourite orange shorts and a pair of white sandals. I'm so worried. Whatever can have happened to her?" sobbed Mrs Richards.
"I'm sure we will find her soon, Mrs Richards," said the sergeant reassuringly. "Your excellent description will help us."

Now see if you can pick out the useful information, and write notes that will help the police to find Ella.

Nine year old girl named Ella Richards.
Last seen on beach near pier.
Tall with dark hair in ponytail. Brown eyes.
Wearing bright green flowered t-shirt, white sandals and orange shorts.

It doesn't matter what order the notes are in as long as all the important facts are there.

Number 38 — Homework Today

Name: Date:

Roman Britain Crossword

How much do you know about the Romans? Using the words in the box to help you, answer the clues to solve my Roman Britain crossword.

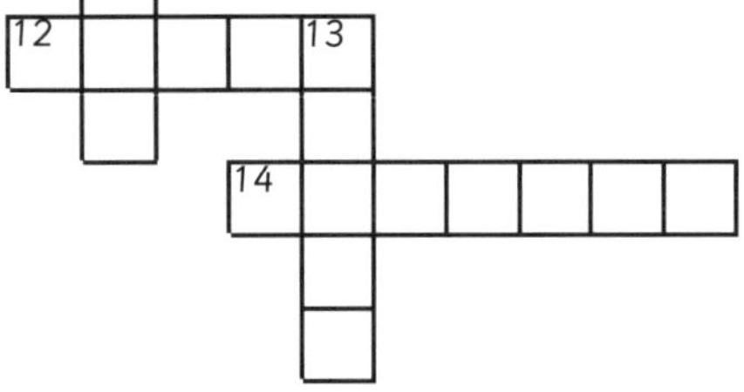

Clues across
1. Romans used these for health and cleanliness.
2. Country of origin of Romans.
3. Picture made from tiny bits of tile.
6. Wall built across northern England.
9. Title of Roman leader.
11. The Romans did this to Britain.
12. People living in Britain before the Romans invaded.
14. Roman Emperor (the wall was named after him).

Clues down
1. Female Celtic leader who fought Romans.
4. Roman officer in charge of 100 men.
5. Usually pulled by two horses.
7. People this crossword is about.
8. About 5,000 foot soldiers = one _________.
10. What the Romans did when they invaded and conquered.
13. Person 'owned' by another person.

Hadrian's Wall	Celts	mosaic	Boudicca	chariot	Romans	
Hadrian	settled	baths	Emperor	invaded	Italy	slave
centurion	legion					

Homework Today — Answer Sheet

Number **38**

Name: Date:

Roman Britain Crossword

How much do you know about the Romans? Using the words in the box to help you, answer the clues to solve my Roman Britain crossword.

Clues across

1. Romans used these for health and cleanliness.
2. Country of origin of Romans.
3. Picture made from tiny bits of tile.
6. Wall built across northern England.
9. Title of Roman leader.
11. The Romans did this to Britain.
12. People living in Britain before the Romans invaded.
14. Roman Emperor (the wall was named after him).

Clues down

1. Female Celtic leader who fought Romans.
4. Roman officer in charge of 100 men.
5. Usually pulled by two horses.
7. People this crossword is about.
8. About 5,000 foot soldiers = one _________.
10. What the Romans did when they invaded and conquered.
13. Person 'owned' by another person.

Hadrian's Wall	Celts	mosaic	Boudicca	chariot	Romans	
Hadrian	settled	baths	Emperor	invaded	Italy	slave
centurion	legion					

Number 39

Homework Today

Name: Date:

World Religions

The words in the word bank are all associated with religions. Please sort them into the correct boxes. Some words may fit in more than one box.

Mohammed Bible Holi Buddhist Jesus bar mitzvah
Hindu Torah Qur'an Makkah Easter temple
Christmas puja rabbi Shema mandir kanga Sikh
turban Jew kirpan nirvana kaaba mosque
Menorah Diwali parable Guru church Muslim
gurdwara om Christian Buddha Allah kara
Pesach (Passover) noble eightfold path

Buddhism

Christianity

Hinduism

Islam

Judaism

Sikhism

Homework Today   Answer Sheet

Number 39

Name: Date:

World Religions

The words in the word bank are all associated with religions. Please sort them into the correct boxes. Some words may fit in more than one box.

Mohammed   Bible   Holi   Buddhist   Jesus   bar mitzvah
Hindu   Torah   Qur'an   Makkah   Easter   temple
Christmas   puja   rabbi   Shema   mandir   kanga   Sikh
turban   Jew   kirpan   nirvana   kaaba   mosque
Menorah   Diwali   parable   Guru   church   Muslim
gurdwara   om   Christian   Buddha   Allah   kara
Pesach (Passover)   noble eightfold path

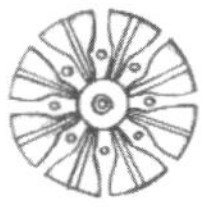

Buddhism

Buddhist   nirvana
Buddha   temple
noble eightfold path

Christianity

parable   Christian
Christmas   Jesus
Bible   Easter
church

Hinduism

mandir   Diwali
Hindu   om   puja
Holi   temple

Islam

Mohammed
Muslim   Allah
Qur'an   Makkah
mosque   kaaba

Judaism

Menorah   Jew
rabbi   Torah
Shema
Pesach (Passover)
bar mitzvah

Sikhism

Guru   temple   Sikh
gurdwara   turban
kara   kirpan

Number

40

Homework Today

Name: Date:

Understanding Music (1)

Millions of people in many countries read and write music in the same way so that they can understand each other's work. You can learn a little about it on this page.

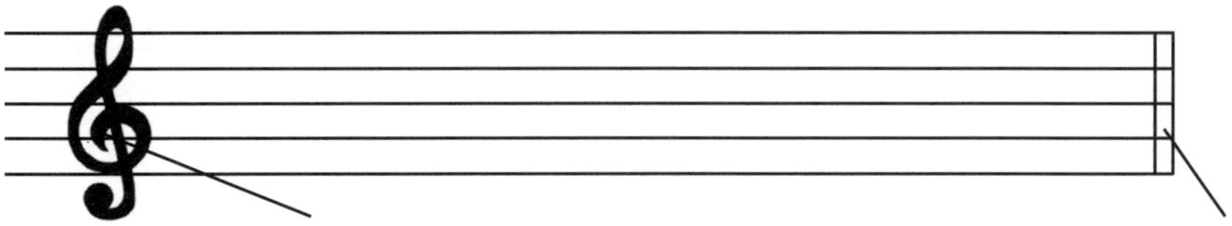

This sign is called a treble clef. Practise drawing it along the stave (set of five lines). Go over mine and then do some more of your own.

This is a double bar line. It shows where the music ends.

Look at these notes and their values.

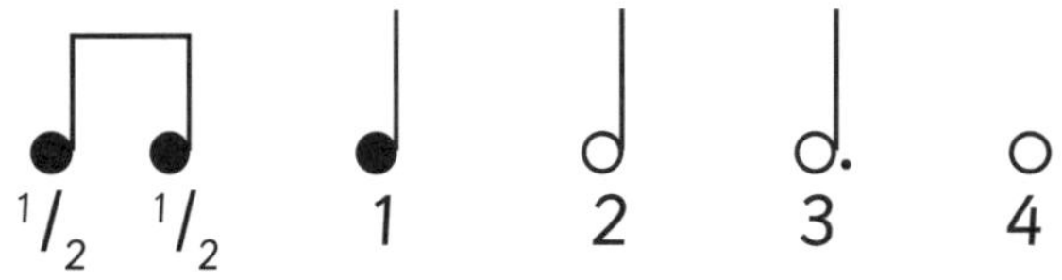

On this line of music there is a 'bar line' after each four beats. Write the note length under each note. I have started it for you.

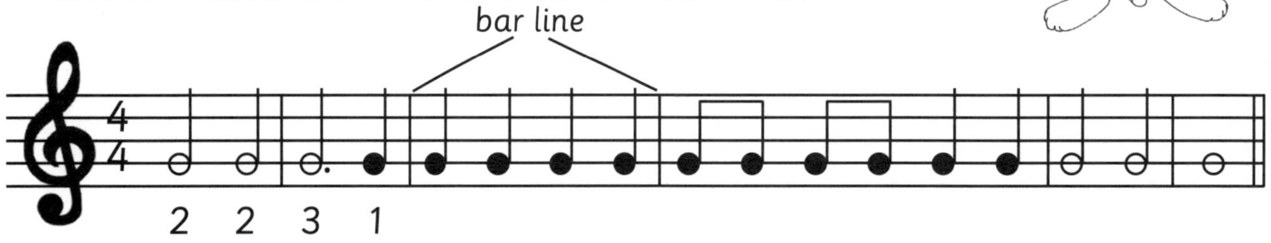

On the next stave put a bar line after each four beats, and write the note length under each note. I have started it for you.

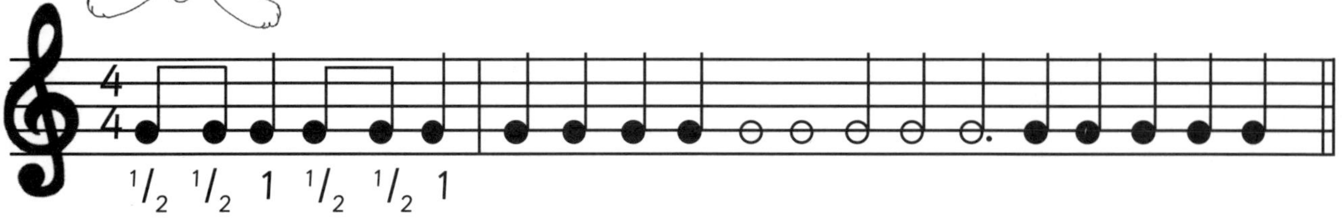

Homework Today Answer Sheet

Number 40

Name: Date:

Understanding Music (1)

Millions of people in many countries read and write music in the same way so that they can understand each other's work. You can learn a little about it on this page.

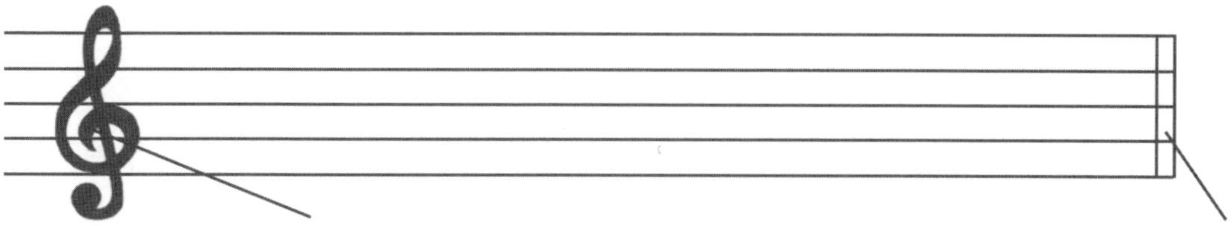

This sign is called a treble clef. Practise drawing it along the stave (set of five lines). Go over mine and then do some more of your own.

This is a double bar line. It shows where the music ends.

Look at these notes and their values.

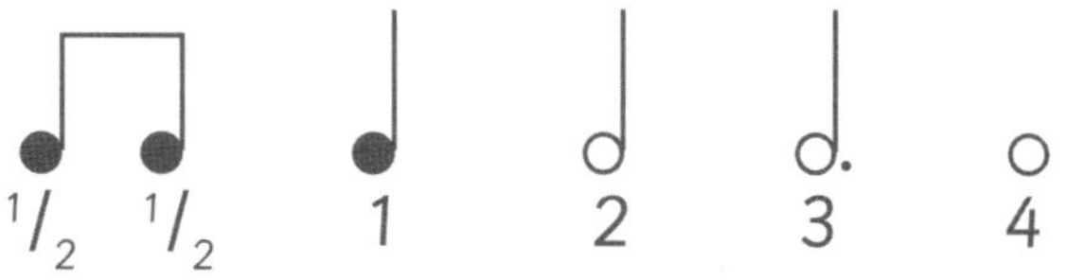

On this line of music there is a 'bar line' after each four beats. Write the note length under each note. I have started it for you.

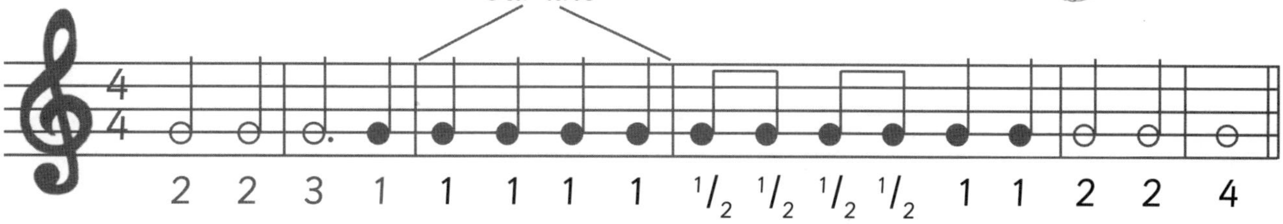

On the next stave put a bar line after each four beats, and write the note length under each note. I have started it for you.

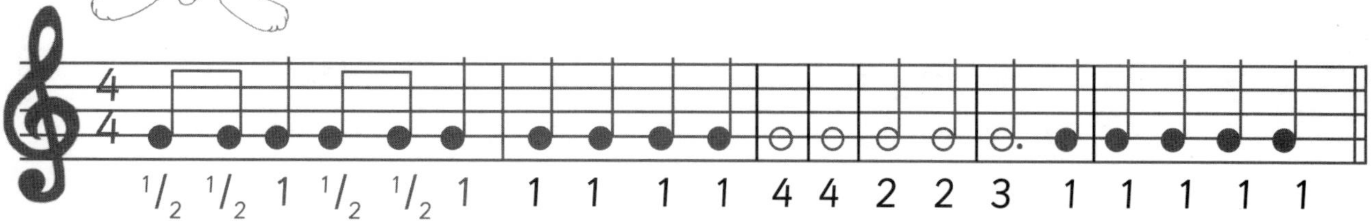

Number 41

Homework Today

Name: Date:

Understanding Music (2)

Now you understand a little bit about how to write music, it's time to learn a little more.

Remember these things:

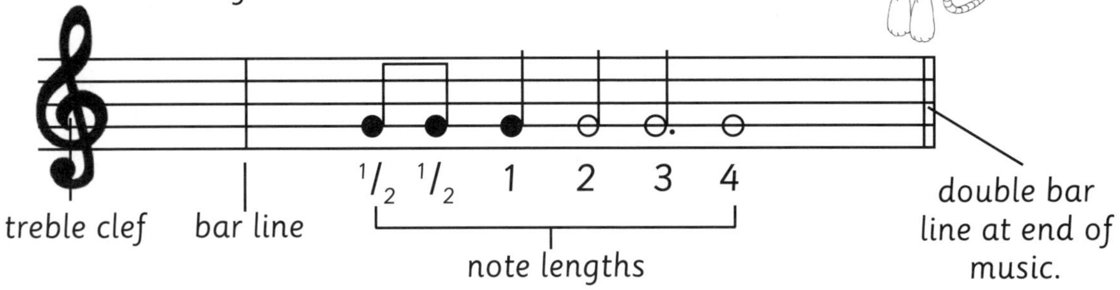

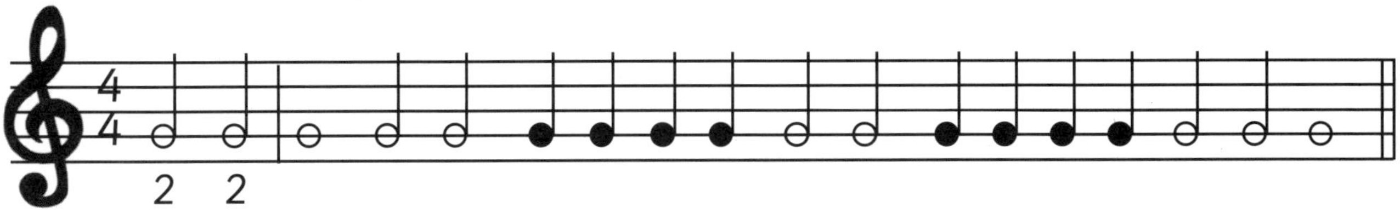

The pair of numbers at the beginning is called a time signature. The top number tells you how many beats are in each bar. On this line of music there are four beats in each bar. Write the note lengths beneath the notes and put in the bar lines. I have started it for you.

This sign indicates a 'rest' (silence): 

Write the note lengths under these rhythm patterns and see if you can clap the rhythms.

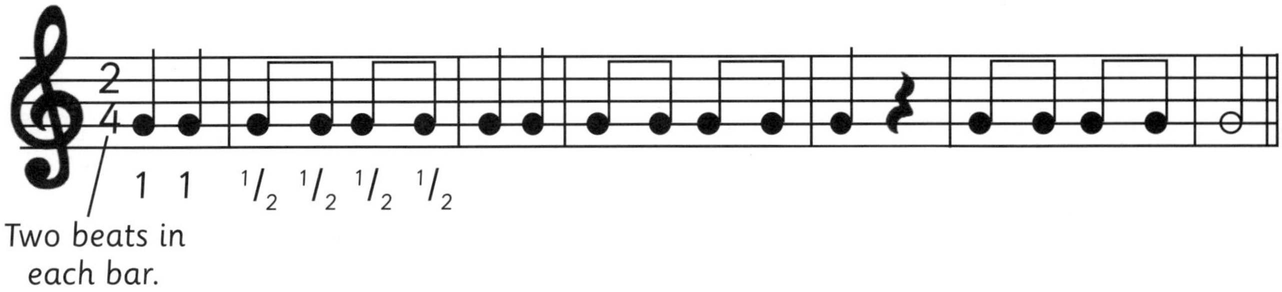

Name: Date:

Understanding Music (2)

Now you understand a little bit about how to write music, it's time to learn a little more.

Remember these things:

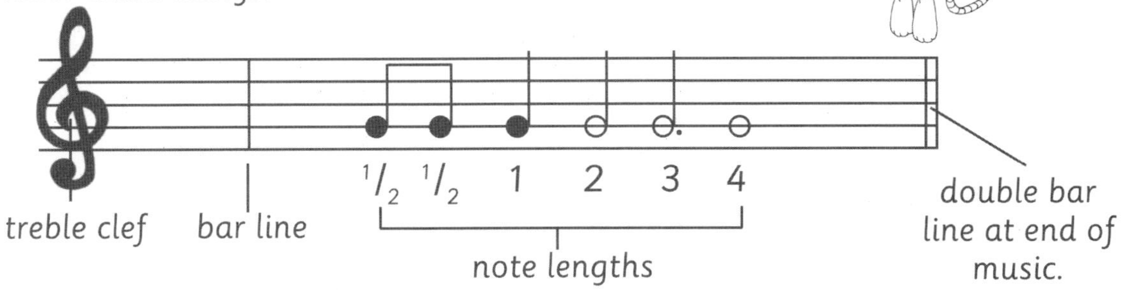

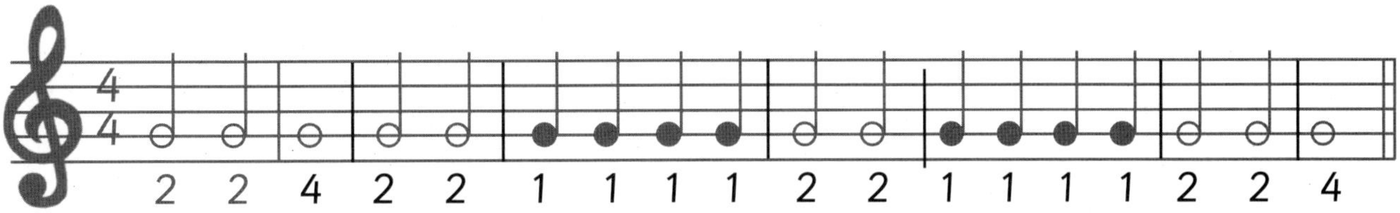

The pair of numbers at the beginning is called a time signature. The top number tells you how many beats are in each bar. On this line of music there are four beats in each bar. Write the note lengths beneath the notes and put in the bar lines. I have started it for you.

This sign indicates a 'rest' (silence): 

Write the note lengths under these rhythm patterns and see if you can clap the rhythms.

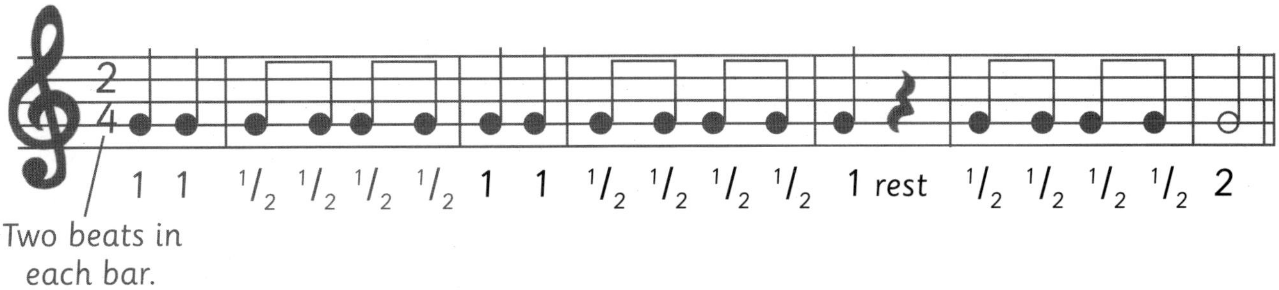

Name: Date:

Music (Exploring Sounds)

Playing different instruments in different ways can remind us of things. Fluttering notes from a flute might make you think of twittering birds.

Look at the list of instruments and the list of sounds and draw lines to match them well. There are no absolutely right or wrong answers as we all have different ideas. You may use one instrument for more than one sound. You do not have to use all the instruments, but you must use all the sounds.

Instruments	Sounds
violin	A clown.
trombone	Fierce dog.
drums	A shoal of fish.
piano	Chattering monkeys.
tambourine	A gliding swan.
guitar	Soldiers marching.
xylophone	A sleepy summer day.
flute	A swooping, soaring bird.

Now give reasons for one of your choices and say how the instrument should be played (slowly, quickly, high or low notes etc.).

____

____

____

____

____

Homework Today Answer Sheet

Number **42**

Name: Date:

Music (Exploring Sounds)

Playing different instruments in different ways can remind us of things. Fluttering notes from a flute might make you think of twittering birds.

Look at the list of instruments and the list of sounds and draw lines to match them well. There are no absolutely right or wrong answers as we all have different ideas. You may use one instrument for more than one sound. You do not have to use all the instruments, but you must use all the sounds.

Possible answers might be:

Instruments	Sounds
violin	A clown.
trombone	Fierce dog.
drums	A shoal of fish.
piano	Chattering monkeys.
tambourine	A gliding swan.
guitar	Soldiers marching.
xylophone	A sleepy summer day.
flute	A swooping, soaring bird.

Now give reasons for one of your choices and say how the instrument should be played (slowly, quickly, high or low notes etc.).

Sample answer

Fast high tinkling notes played quite quietly on a piano would remind me of a shoal of fish swimming along in the sea.

Number 43

Homework Today

Name: Date:

Types of Words

Read the following information carefully, it will help you with this work.

Nouns	are naming words,	eg: house.
Verbs	are doing words,	eg: climb.
Adverbs	show how a verb is done,	eg: quickly.
Pronouns	can be used in place of nouns,	eg: it.
Adjectives	can be used to describe nouns,	eg: big.

Sort the words from the word bank below into the correct containers.

house green them slowly they sadly car huge shoe
tiny it jump happily drive stand brilliantly climb he
run cow dog juicy yellow crunchy television step
laugh paper she carefully river amazingly these
quickly large

nouns

pronouns

adjectives

verbs

adverbs

Homework Today　　Answer Sheet

Number 43

Name:　　　　　　Date:

Types of Words

Read the following information carefully, it will help you with this work.

<u>Nouns</u>	are naming words,	eg: house.
<u>Verbs</u>	are doing words,	eg: climb.
<u>Adverbs</u>	show how a verb is done,	eg: quickly.
<u>Pronouns</u>	can be used in place of nouns,	eg: it.
<u>Adjectives</u>	can be used to describe nouns,	eg: big.

Sort the words from the word bank below into the correct containers.

house green them slowly they sadly car huge shoe tiny it jump happily drive stand brilliantly climb he run cow dog juicy yellow crunchy television step laugh paper she carefully river amazingly these quickly large

<u>nouns</u>

house car shoe cow dog paper river television

<u>pronouns</u>

them they it he she these

<u>adjectives</u>

green huge tiny juicy large yellow crunchy

<u>verbs</u>

jump drive stand climb run stop laugh

<u>adverbs</u>

slowly sadly happily brilliantly amazingly quickly carefully

Number 44

Homework Today

Name: Date:

Verb Tenses

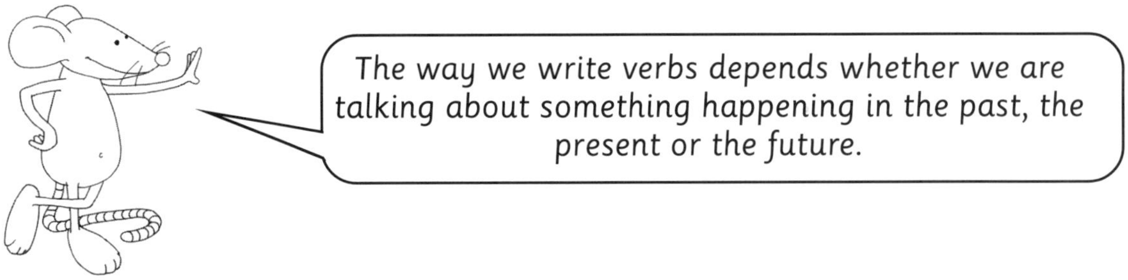

Complete the chart below. The first word has been done for you.

PAST	PRESENT	FUTURE
I ran	I am running	I will run
You walked		
	They are hobbling	
We needed		
He hoped		
		I will go

Rewrite each of the following sentences to change their tense.

Present → I am skipping along the road to school.

Past → ______________________________

Future → Soon I will be going on holiday.

Past → ______________________________

Past → On my birthday I went to the cinema.

Future → ______________________________

Homework Today   Answer Sheet

Number 44

Name: Date:

Verb Tenses

The way we write verbs depends whether we are talking about something happening in the past, the present or the future.

Complete the chart below. The first word has been done for you.

PAST	PRESENT	FUTURE
I ran	I am running	I will run
You walked	You are walking	You will walk
They hobbled	They are hobbling	They will hobble
We needed	We need	We will need
He hoped	He is hoping	He will hope
I went	I am going	I will go

Rewrite each of the following sentences to change their tense.

Present → I am skipping along the road to school.

Past → I skipped along the road to school.

Future → Soon I will be going on holiday.

Past → I went on holiday.

Past → On my birthday I went to the cinema.

Future → On my birthday I will be going to the cinema.

Number

45

Homework Today

Name: Date:

Using Apostrophes

When words are singular we can use an apostrophe before the 's' to show that something belongs to them.

Put an apostrophe in each of the following sentences. The first one is done for you.

The dog's bone is on the grass. (The bone belongs to the dog.)

Matthews books are very good.

The farmers tractor needs mending.

The doctors patients are waiting to be seen.

Now make up a sentence of your own where the singular noun needs an apostrophe before the 's'.

If the noun is plural, the apostrophe must go **after** the 's' to show belonging.

Put the apostrophe in the correct place in the following sentences to show that the noun is plural. The first one is done for you.

The dogs' bones are on the grass. (The bones belong to the dogs.)

The boys books are very good. (More than one boy.)

The farmers tractors need mending. (More than one farmer.)

The doctors patients are waiting to be seen. (More than one doctor.)

Now make up a sentence of your own where the 'plural' noun needs an apostrophe after the 's'.

Homework Today Answer Sheet

Number **45**

Name: Date:

Using Apostrophes

When words are singular we can use an apostrophe before the 's' to show that something belongs to them.

Put an apostrophe in each of the following sentences. The first one is done for you.

The dog's bone is on the grass. (The bone belongs to the dog)

Matthew's books are very good.

The farmer's tractor needs mending.

The doctor's patients are waiting to be seen.

Now make up a sentence of your own where the singular noun needs an apostrophe before the 's'.

This sentence will be individual to the pupil.

If the noun is plural, the apostrophe must go **after** the 's' to show belonging.

Put the apostrophe in the correct place in the following sentences to show that the noun is plural. The first one is done for you.

The dogs' bones are on the grass. (The bones belong to the dogs.)

The boys' books are very good. (More than one boy.)

The farmers' tractors need mending. (More than one farmer.)

The doctors' patients are waiting to be seen. (More than one doctor.)

Now make up a sentence of your own where the 'plural' noun needs an apostrophe after the 's'.

This sentence will be individual to the pupil.

Number 46

Homework Today

Name: Date:

The View from the Window

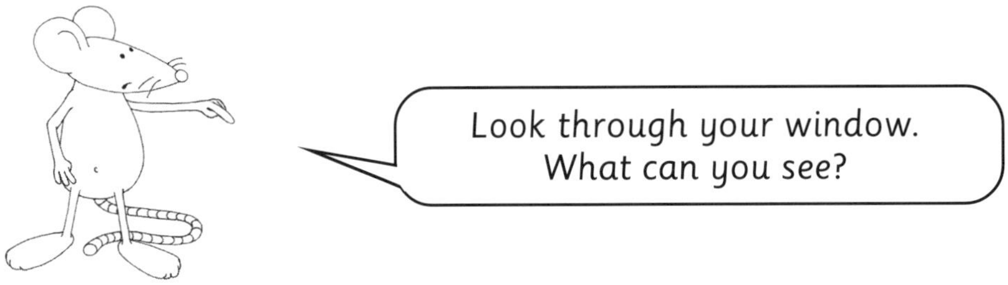

Try to draw your view in the box below. You should step back and draw exactly what you see framed by the window.

Describe your view. What do you like or dislike about it? What buildings and plants can you see? What else can you see?

Homework Today Answer Sheet

Number 46

Name: Date:

The View from the Window

Look through your window.
What can you see?

Try to draw your view in the box below. You should step back and draw exactly what you see framed by the window.

The drawing will be individual to each pupil and will depend on their location.

Describe your view. What do you like or dislike about it? What buildings and plants can you see? What else can you see?

This description will be individual to each pupil and will depend on their location.

Number 47

Homework Today

Name: Date:

Map of a Garden

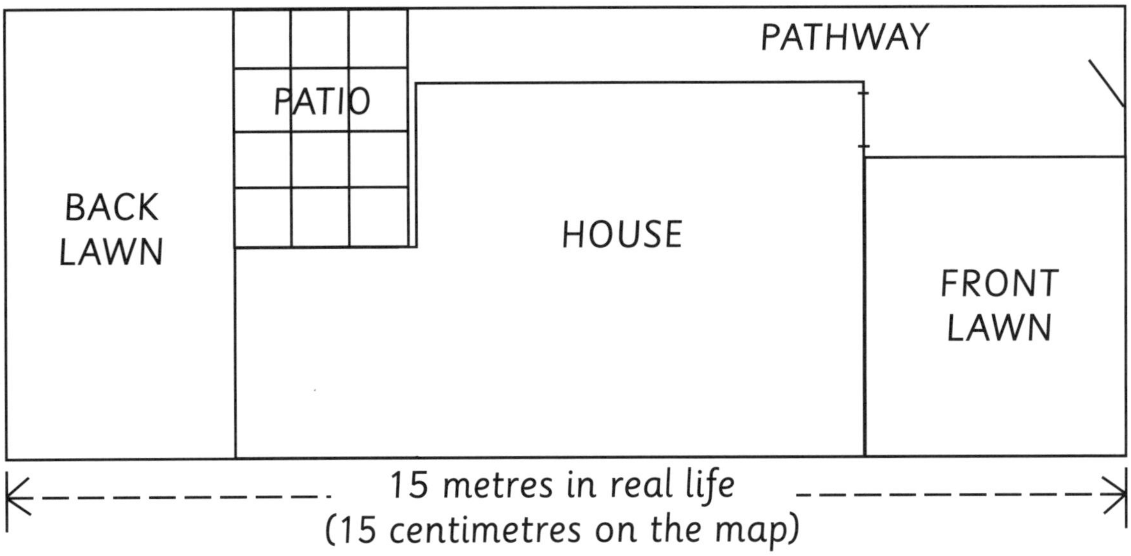

One centimetre on the map is worth one metre in real life.

We say that the scale is one centimetre to one metre.

Use a ruler to measure the map carefully when you answer these questions:

	On the map	In real life
1. How wide is the back lawn?		
2. How long is the back lawn?		
3. How far is the front door from the garden gate?		
4. How wide is the path next to the house?		
5. The patio is made of square slabs. How long are the sides of each slab?		

Now colour the map:

Make the lawns green.
Make the patio grey.
Make the house red.
Make the path brown.

Homework Today Answer Sheet

Number 47

Name: Date:

Map of a Garden

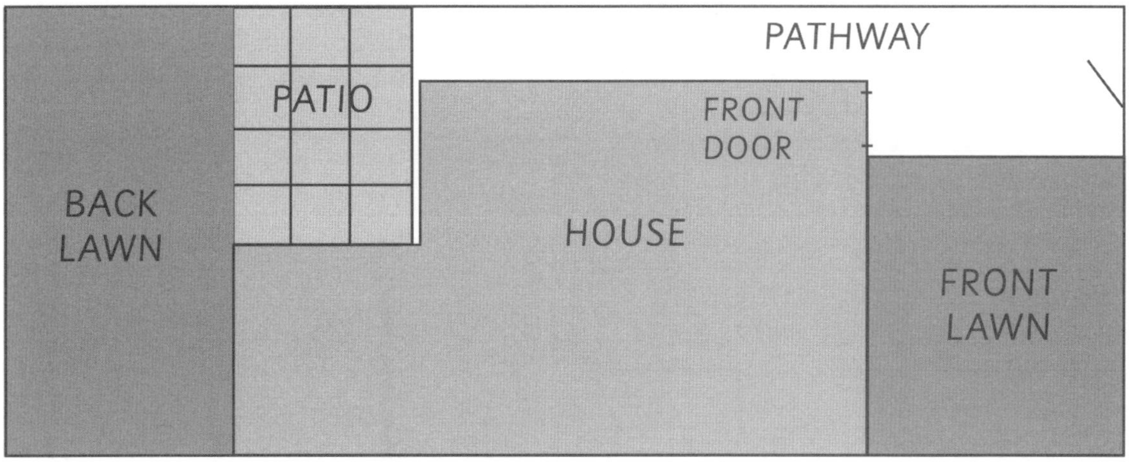

15 metres in real life
(15 centimetres on the map)

One centimetre on the map is worth one metre in real life.

We say that the scale is one centimetre to one metre.

Use a ruler to measure the map carefully when you answer these questions:

		On the map	In real life
1.	How wide is the back lawn?	3 cm	3 m
2.	How long is the back lawn?	6 cm	6 m
3.	How far is the front door from the garden gate?	3.5 cm	3.5 m
4.	How wide is the path next to the house?	1 cm	1 m
5.	The patio is made of square slabs. How long are the sides of each slab?	.8 cm	.8 m

Now colour the map:

Make the lawns green. Make the house red.
Make the patio grey. Make the path brown.

Number

48

Homework Today

Name: Date:

Thermometers

The first thermometer on the right shows a temperature of 14 degrees Celsius. We write 14 °C.

What temperatures do the other thermometers on the right show?

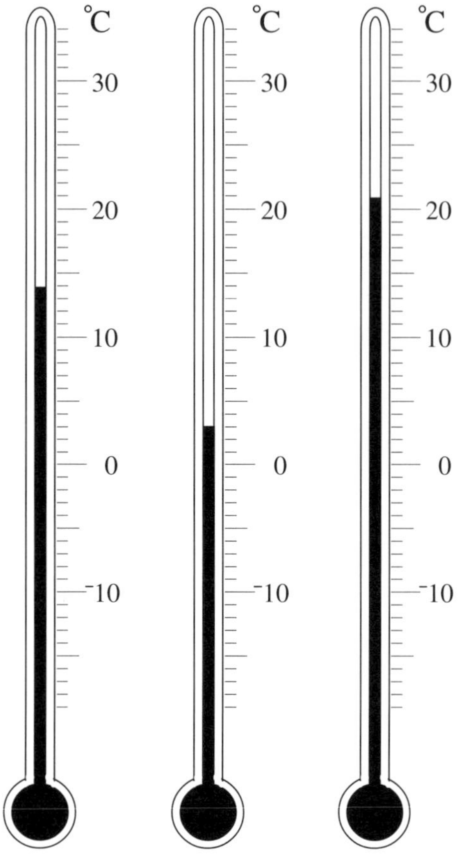

14 °C

Draw liquid in the thermometers on the left to show the temperature given.

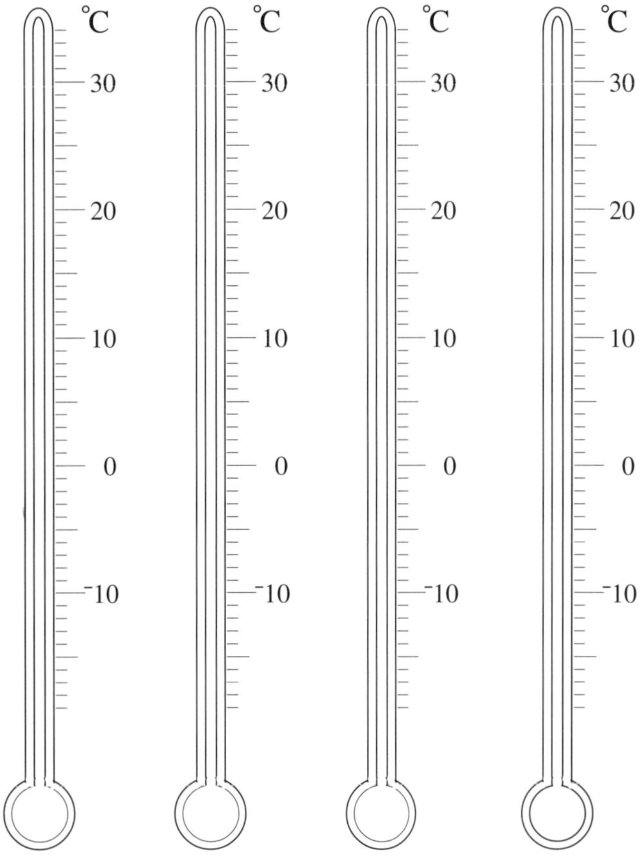

11 °C 6 °C 0 °C -2 °C

Watch the weather forecast. What temperature is expected for your area tomorrow?

Homework Today — Answer Sheet

Number 48

Name: Date:

Thermometers

The first thermometer on the right shows a temperature of 14 degrees Celsius. We write 14 °C.

What temperatures do the other thermometers on the right show?

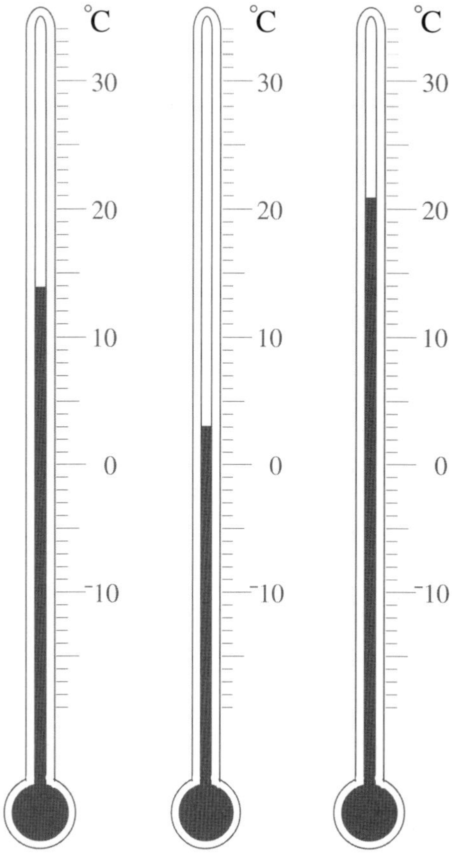

14 °C   3 °C   21 °C

Draw liquid in the thermometers on the left to show the temperature given.

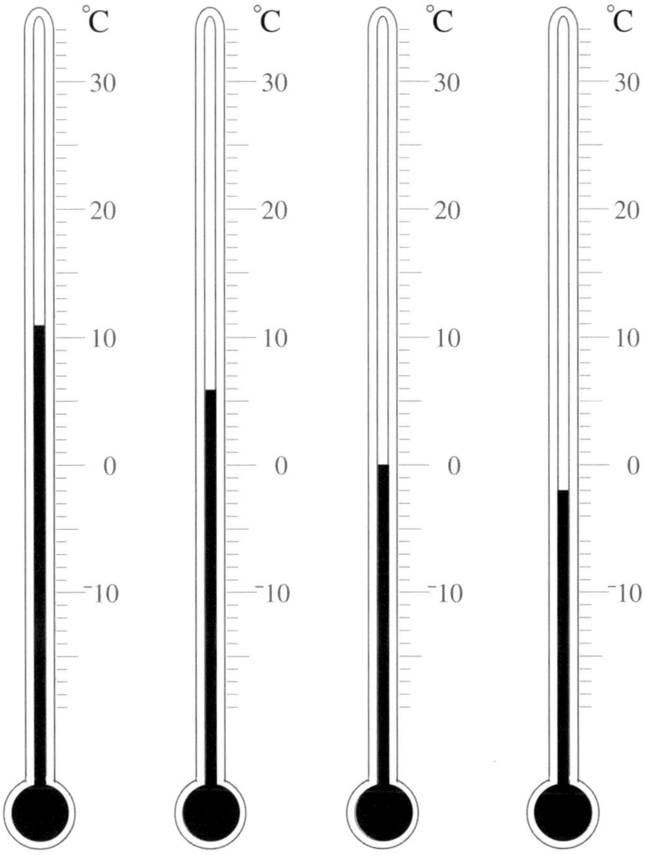

11 °C   6 °C   0 °C   -2 °C

Watch the weather forecast. What temperature is expected for your area tomorrow?

Number 49

Homework Today

Name: Date:

Arms

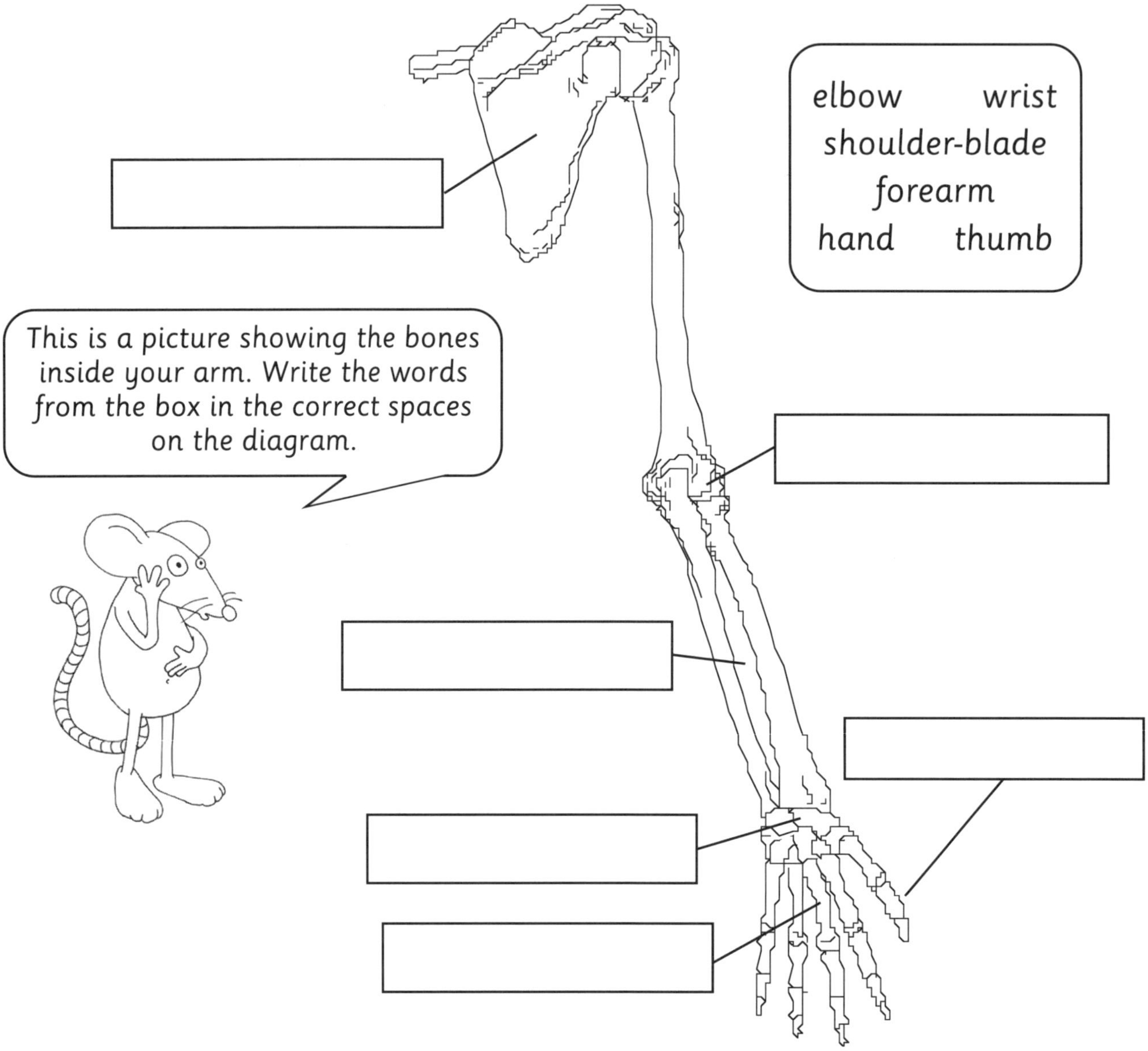

Now work with an adult.

Measure your forearm from the elbow to the wrist. How long is it?

Measure an adult's forearm. How long is it?

Which forearm is longer?

By how much longer is it?

Homework Today — Answer Sheet

Number 49

Name: Date:

Arms

This is a picture showing the bones inside your arm. Write the words from the box in the correct spaces on the diagram.

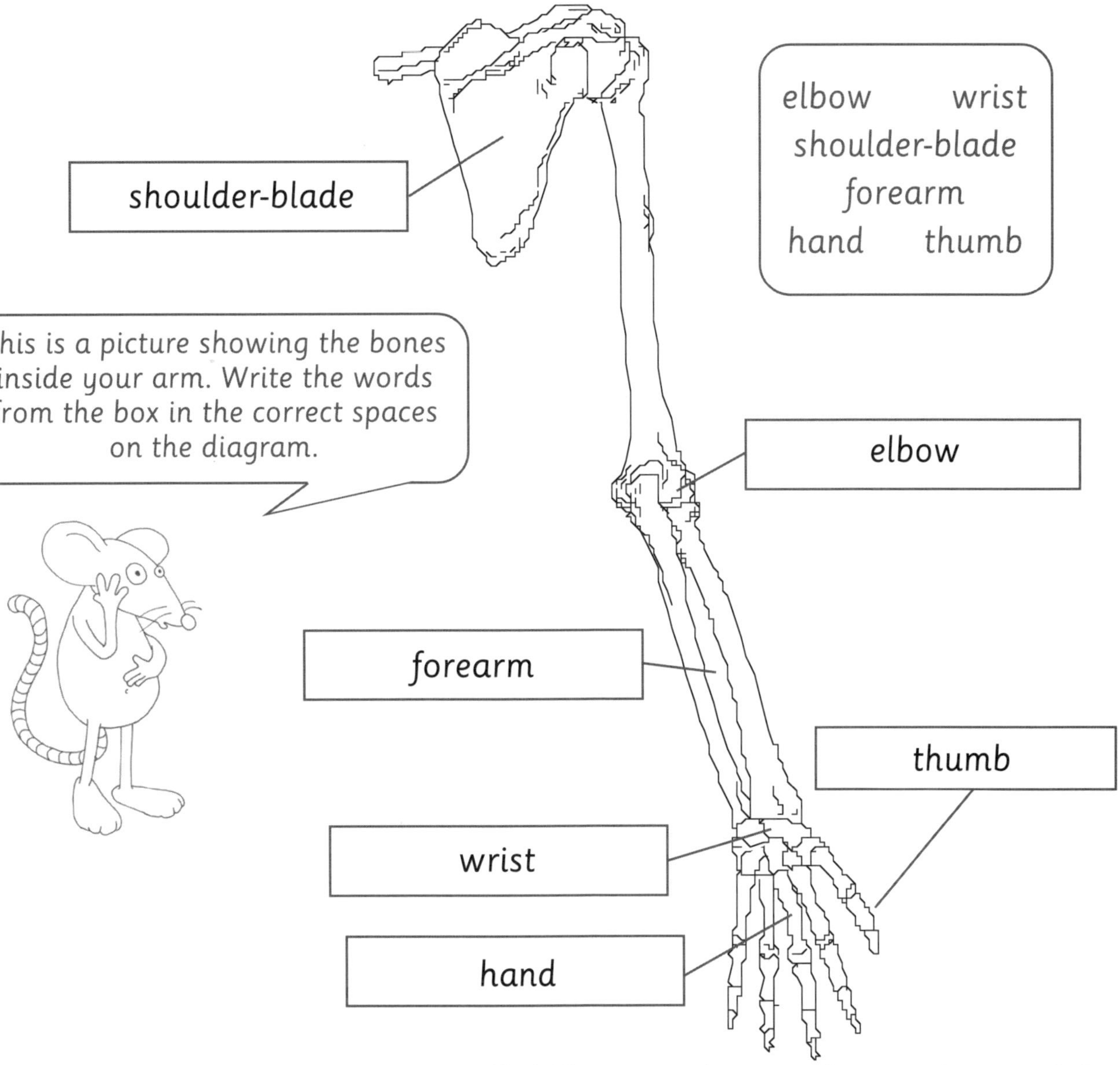

The answers to these questions will differ according to the pupil and adult that they measure.

Measure your forearm from the elbow to the wrist. How long is it?

Measure an adult's forearm. How long is it?

Which forearm is longer?

By how much longer is it?

Number

50

Homework Today

Name: Date:

Hands

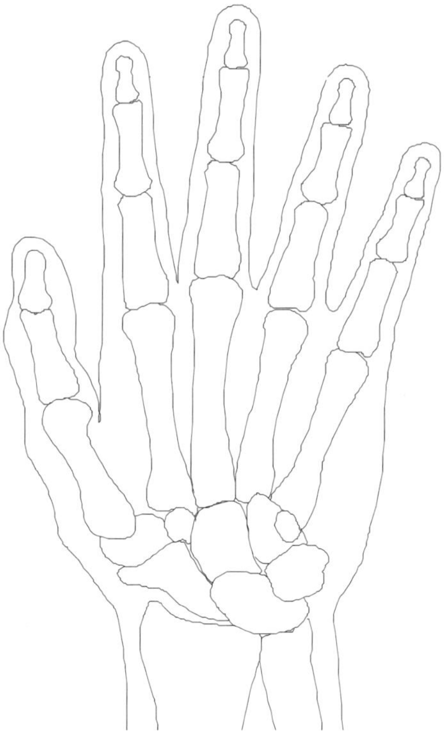

Are there more than fifteen or less than fifteen bones in the hand?

Measure your hand from your wrist to the tip of your longest finger.

How long is it?

Now measure an adult's hand.

How long is it?

Measure an adult's hand-span. This is the distance between the tip of the little finger and the tip of the thumb when the hand is stretched as wide as possible.

How wide is it?

Who has the biggest hand in your house?

Who has the smallest hand?

Homework Today   Answer Sheet

Number 50

Name: Date:

Hands

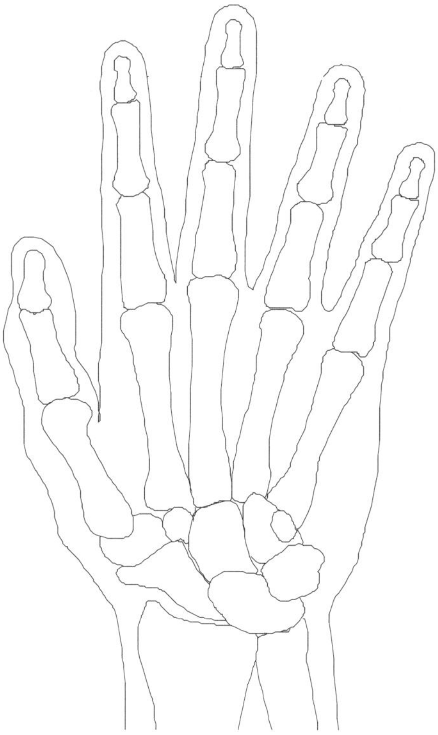

The answers to these questions will differ according to the pupil and adult that they measure.

Are there more than fifteen or less than fifteen bones in the hand?

More than fifteen.

Measure your hand from your wrist to the tip of your longest finger.

How long is it?

Now measure an adult's hand.

How long is it?

Measure an adult's hand-span. This is the distance between the tip of the little finger and the tip of the thumb when the hand is stretched as wide as possible.

How wide is it?

Who has the biggest hand in your house?

Who has the smallest hand?

HOMEWORK TODAY *for ages 8-9*
Individual Record Sheet

Name:	Sheet	Date completed	Comment by parent / pupil / teacher.
Words and Numbers	1		
Numbers in Order	2		
Number Lines	3		
Positive and Negative	4		
Addition Bonds	5		
Quick Subtractions	6		
Addition Pairs	7		
More Addition Pairs	8		
Quick Doubles	9		
More Doubles	10		
Quick Halves	11		
Shapes and Perimeters	12		
Using a Ruler	13		
Using Measuring Cylinders	14		
Area	15		
More Area	16		
Centuries	17		
Months of the Year	18		
Minutes, Hours and Days	19		
A Bar-chart	20		
Rhyming Couplets	21		
Alliteration	22		
Alphabetical Order	23		
Double Consonants	24		
More Rhyming Couplets	25		
Nouns, Adjectives and Verbs	26		
Adverbs	27		
Alphabetical Animals	28		
Gender Words	29		
Comparative Adjectives	30		
Building a Character	31		
Describing a Character	32		
Turning Notes into Prose	33		
Technical Vocabulary	34		
Pyramid Puzzle	35		
Now and Then	36		
Turning Prose into Notes	37		
Roman Britain Crossword	38		
World Religions	39		
Understanding Music (1)	40		
Understanding Music (2)	41		
Music (Exploring Sounds)	42		
Types of Words	43		
Verb Tenses	44		
Using Apostrophes	45		
The View from the Window	46		
Map of a Garden	47		
Thermometers	48		
Arms	49		
Hands	50		